CAMPAIGN 433

WESTPORT 1864

Price's Raid and the Midwest's Greatest Battle

BRIAN LANE HERDER ILLUSTRATED BY MARCO CAPPARONI

OSPREY PUBLISHING
Bloomsbury Publishing Plc
Kemp House, Chawley Park, Cumnor Hill, Oxford OX2 9PH, UK
Bloomsbury Publishing Ireland Limited,
29 Earlsfort Terrace, Dublin 2, D02 AY28, Ireland
Bloomsbury Publishing Inc.
1359 Broadway, 12th Floor, New York, NY 10018, USA
E-mail: info@ospreypublishing.com
www.ospreypublishing.com

OSPREY is a trademark of Osprey Publishing Ltd

First published in Great Britain in 2026

A catalog record for this book is available from the British Library.

ISBN: PB 9781472871244; eBook 9781472871251; ePDF 9781472871220; XML 9781472871237

26 27 28 29 30 10 9 8 7 6 5 4 3 2 1

Maps by Bounford.com
3D BEV by Paul Kime
Index by Fionbar Lyons
Typeset by Lumina Datamatics Ltd
Printed by Repro India Ltd

MIX
Paper
FSC FSC® C047271

Osprey Publishing supports the Woodland Trust, the UK's leading woodland conservation charity.

To find out more about our authors and books visit **www.ospreypublishing.com**. Here you will find extracts, author interviews, details of forthcoming events and the option to sign up for our newsletter.

For product safety related questions contact productsafety@ bloomsbury.com

Dedication

Westport 1864 is dedicated to my 4-year-old son, Alexander Dawson Herder, who just missed meeting his late paternal grandfather, but constantly imagines the adventures they would have had together. They would have loved each other. With the Civil War, the Wild West, the Kansas Jayhawkers, and Kansas City all crammed into the same campaign, I know Alexander's grandfather would also have loved reading *Westport 1864*; there is no doubt that the three of us Kansas boys would have sure enjoyed exploring this Jayhawker story together.

List of acronyms

EMM	Enrolled Missouri Militia
KSM	Kansas State Militia
MSG	Missouri State Guard
MSM	Missouri State Militia
PEMM	Provisional Enrolled Missouri Militia

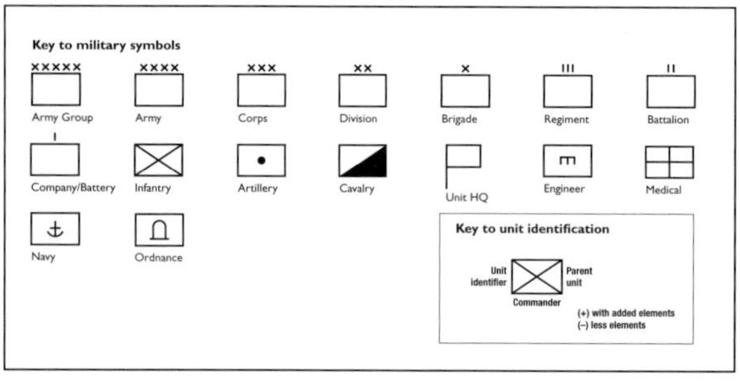

Front cover main illustration: The last stand of the 2nd Kansas State Militia at Mockbee Farm, 1545hrs, October 22, 1864. (Marco Capparoni)
Title page photograph: Battle of the Big Blue River, October 22, 1864. (kansasmemory.org, Kansas State Historical Society)

CONTENTS

ORIGINS OF THE CAMPAIGN 4

Introduction ▪ Kansas and Missouri, 1854–61 ▪ Confederate actions in Missouri, 1861–63 ▪ The Kansas–Missouri Border War, 1861–64 ▪ The strategic situation, 1864

CHRONOLOGY 21

OPPOSING COMMANDERS 24

Confederate ▪ Federal

OPPOSING FORCES 28

Confederate ▪ Federal ▪ Orders of battle

OPPOSING PLANS 34

Weather and terrain ▪ Confederate ▪ Federal

THE CAMPAIGN 37

Price's Army of Missouri departs, August 28–September 19 ▪ Price invades Missouri, September 20–October 7 ▪ Missouri bushwhacker actions, July 23–October 9 ▪ The race to Kansas, October 8–21 ▪ The battle of Westport, October 22–23 ▪ The Federal pursuit, October 24–28

AFTERMATH 91

THE BATTLEFIELDS TODAY 93

SELECT BIBLIOGRAPHY 94

INDEX 95

ORIGINS OF THE CAMPAIGN

INTRODUCTION

Today, Westport is a quiet neighborhood in Kansas City, Missouri. However, in 1864, it was the site of the climactic, decisive battle in the complex, decade-long "Border War" that convulsed the US states of Kansas and Missouri – a time and place when the American Civil War and the American Wild West blurred to indistinguishability.

Price's Raid, culminating at the October 22–23, 1864 battle of Westport, was one of the largest cavalry raids of the war by size and distance. It was the Confederacy's last invasion of the Union, and indeed was the Confederacy's last strategic offensive of any kind. The 30,000 men who fought at Westport makes it the largest Civil War battle fought west of the Mississippi and the largest battle ever fought in the modern-day Midwest. The ensuing battle of Mine Creek, fought in southeast Kansas two days later, would prove the war's second-largest cavalry battle.

The Old Westport sign seen in 2010. Westport was annexed by the rapidly growing Kansas City in 1897. By 2026, Kansas City was the largest single city in the state of Missouri, and the second-largest metropolitan area after St. Louis. (Iknowthegoods, CC BY-SA 3.0 https://creativecommons.org/licenses/by-sa/3.0, via Wikimedia Commons)

Despite its obscurity, Westport and its wider campaign are distinguished by an astonishingly rich roster of celebrated 19th-century American personalities, all of whom either were already or were destined to become famous for events other than Westport. Among those involved in the campaign who would achieve later fame (or infamy) as Wild West icons were William "Buffalo Bill" Cody, James "Wild Bill" Hickok, mountain man Jeremiah "Liver-Eating" Johnson, Lieutenant Colonel Frederick Benteen (Custer's future battalion commander at Little Big Horn), and outlaw siblings Jesse James and Frank James. Appearing near the end of their murderous careers were the James' infamous ringleaders, Missouri bushwhackers William "Bloody Bill" Anderson and William C. Quantrill. Their lawless pro-Union counterpart

Price's Westport campaign, August–December 1864

Charles R. "Doc" Jennison, a Kansas "redleg," commanded a cavalry brigade at Westport – "Jennison's Jayhawkers." Jennison was joined at Westport by two fellow Kansas Jayhawker colonels – James H. Montgomery, former 2nd South Carolina Colored Volunteers commander, and the mercurial demagogue James H. "Jim" Lane, the state's contemporary US senator to Congress. Indeed, Westport boasted a veritable constellation of politically minded military officers, including one prewar state governor, four postwar state governors, and four postwar US senators. The following year, a more obscure Westport veteran, James H. Ford, would order the establishment of western Kansas' Fort Dodge – the future Dodge City.

Additionally, Missouri was a backwater for prominent cast-off Federal generals who had fallen out of political favor farther East. The campaign's highest-ranking Federal commander was Major General William Rosecrans, former commander of the Army of the Cumberland, while Rosecrans' Federal cavalry was commanded by Major General Alfred Pleasonton, architect of the entire wartime US Cavalry branch, and the man who would win the distinction of leading the Union at the Civil War's largest cavalry battles in both the East and the West (Brandy Station and Mine Creek). The most famous and capable Confederate general at Westport was undoubtedly Brigadier General Joseph "Jo" Shelby of the celebrated Iron Brigade. Shelby would go down in history as the "undefeated Confederate," never surrendering to the Union and leading his remnant forces into Mexico to fight on behalf of Emperor Maximilian.

KANSAS AND MISSOURI, 1854–61

The United States purchased virtually the entire center of the North American continent from France in 1803 with the Louisiana Purchase. Among the tract's many vast regions were the future US states of Missouri and Kansas.

By the early 19th century, American national politics was already dominated by the slavery question. Missouri entered the Union as a slave state in 1821, paired with the free state of Maine and the result of the 1820 Missouri Compromise aimed at keeping the US Senate evenly divided between free states and slave states. A key stipulation was that no further slave states would be admitted to the Union north of Missouri's southern border – the 36°30' N parallel. This delicate balancing act of admitting paired free states and slave states according to the 36°30' N parallel endured until 1854. However, powerful complicating political forces had since emerged – a drive for western expansion, the prospect of building a transcontinental railroad, the emergence of anti-slavery Prohibitionists, and a rapidly growing Northern population that increasingly outnumbered that of the South. As the

US troops raise the American flag at New Orleans after taking possession of the Louisiana Purchase from France. The Louisiana Purchase was sold for just $15 million by Napoleon Bonaparte and encompassed parts or all of 15 future US states, including Missouri and Kansas. (Matysik, CC0, via Wikimedia Commons)

South found itself increasingly overwhelmed by Northern demographic superiority, Southern politicians grew frantic to preserve slavery's future and responded by issuing aggressive demands and secession threats in Congress.

Missouri was and remains a geographically and politically heterogeneous state, easily polarized and divided. The Mississippi River defines Missouri's eastern border. The eponymous Missouri River flows from west to east, splitting the state in half before flowing into the Mississippi just north of St. Louis. In 1860, Missouri's slave-owning aristocracy and leading pro-Confederacy sentiment were concentrated along the agriculturally rich Missouri River valley, where Lieutenant General Sterling Price, Major General John Marmaduke, and Brigadier General Joseph "Jo" Shelby all owned plantations. This region, nicknamed "Little Dixie," was where Price expected to most productively recruit Southern sympathizers as he made his way up the Missouri River valley towards Kansas. Jefferson City, the Missouri state capital, was located on the southern bank of the Missouri River almost directly in the center of the state.

Sterling Price was born into a moderately wealthy Virginia slave-owning family in 1809. He would later move to Missouri in 1830 and become a brigadier general in the Mexican War before being elected governor of Missouri between 1853 and 1857. Price died in 1867, just three years after Westport. (Library of Congress, public domain, via Wikimedia Commons)

Missouri's 1861 population was nearly 1.2 million, of whom 77 percent were of Southern heritage and 10 percent – 115,000 – were slaves. Only 40 percent of Missouri's population was born in the state, with another 37 percent born elsewhere in the United States, led by Kentucky, Tennessee, and Virginia. About 23 percent of Missourians were foreign-born, led by Germans and Irish. Indeed, German-Americans in particular would prove strident Unionists in the upcoming war, which would become an issue when Price's army invaded. St. Louis, with a population of 160,000, sat on the Mississippi River and was easily Missouri's largest city and indeed the eighth-largest city in the country. Eastern Missouri was well established; St. Louis' founding preceded the United States' by 12 years, while western Missouri had been the very edge of white settlement until the opening of Kansas Territory in 1854.

Bleeding Kansas, 1854–58

In 1854, the Kansas–Nebraska Act discarded the Missouri Compromise and established the Kansas and Nebraska Territories, stipulating that the territories' settlers would vote on the slavery issue themselves – "popular sovereignty." Unsurprisingly, the settling of Kansas immediately became a race between free-soiler and pro-slavery factions. In this ideologically fueled period, Kansas became a proxy war for the rest of the nation – first politically, and eventually through violence.

In Massachusetts, the state legislature immediately chartered the New England Emigrant Aid Company devoted to settling abolitionists in Kansas to counteract the inevitable pro-slavery invasion. By July 1854, the first group of New England free-soilers, or Free Staters, had arrived in Kansas and founded the abolitionist stronghold of Lawrence. By late 1854, more Free Staters would found the future state capital of Topeka.

The first Kansas elections were scheduled for March 30, 1855. However, neighboring Missourians saw Kansas Territory's rich Missouri and Kansas river valleys as ripe real estate for slave-produced agriculture and therefore

An 1856 map of the United States showing the slave states in gray, free states in pink, and remaining territories in green, with the Kansas Territory not filled in at all. One notices that Kansas Territory then stretched deep into modern-day Colorado before terminating at the Continental Divide in the Rockies; modern Colorado's state capital Denver is named after a Kansas Territory governor. (New York: Wm. C. Reynolds and J. C. Jones, public domain, via Wikimedia Commons)

natural extensions of Missouri's fertile and pro-slavery Little Dixie region. Immediately, Kansas Territory was flooded with armed pro-slavery "Border Ruffians" from Missouri, swamping the polls. Although Kansas had only 1,500 registered voters in 1855, some 6,000 ballots were cast. The illegal Missouri voters thus elected a pro-slavery Kansas government on March 30, 1855. Defiant Free Staters called the new administration the "Bogus Legislature" and refused to recognize it as legitimate. In December 1855, the Kansas Free Staters wrote their own constitution and formed their own legislature. Kansas shortly had two separate territorial governments – a pro-slavery legislature governed by the Lecompton Constitution with its capital in Atchison, and a Free State legislature governed by the Topeka Constitution with its capital in Lawrence.

The nearly bloodless Wakarusa War had already broken out on November 21, 1855, when a pro-slavery settler shot and killed a Free State rival in Douglas County. The incident quickly spiraled out of control. Within days, a pro-slavery army of 1,500 armed Missouri Border Ruffians descended on Lawrence, which was shortly defended by a hastily organized Free State militia of 800 men led by Charles Robinson and Jim Lane. An uneasy siege developed, which was finally ended through negotiation by Kansas Governor Wilson Shannon in December.

By 1856, a Congressional committee had found Kansas' ruling pro-slavery government illegitimate due to massive voter fraud, but President Franklin Pierce, a "doughface" (pro-slavery Northerner), recognized the pro-slavery territorial government anyway. Open warfare quickly broke out, as the Kansas frontier attracted many lawless and violent types. Between 1854 and 1861, about 56 people would be killed in Kansas as a result of

Tragic Prelude, John Steuart Curry's legendary 1942 mural depicting Bleeding Kansas, is on the second floor of the Kansas State Capitol building in Topeka. The central figure is the radical abolitionist John Brown, carrying a rifle in one hand and a Bible in the other. (The Picture Art Collection/Alamy Stock Photo)

politically motivated violence concerning the slavery question, an era called "Bleeding Kansas."

On May 21, 1856, some 850 pro-slavery Missouri Border Ruffians ransacked Lawrence, destroying a hotel and two Free State newspaper presses. The only fatality was a pro-slavery man killed by falling debris. In Washington, DC the following day, South Carolina Congressman Preston Brooks beat Massachusetts Senator Charles Sumner nearly to death over an inflammatory anti-slavery speech Sumner had made two days earlier about Kansas. Back in Kansas, on the night of May 25/26, radical abolitionist John Brown and his four sons, armed with swords, hacked five pro-slavery Kansans to death at Pottawatomie Creek, kicking off a period of violent escalation that would result in 29 dead in three months.

On the order of President Pierce, some 500 US Army troops from Kansas' Fort Leavenworth and Fort Riley converged on the Free State stronghold of Topeka on July 4, 1856. After arming and pointing their cannon at Topeka's Constitution Hall, they ordered the Free State legislature to disperse. Weeks later, in August 1856, Missourian John W. Reid led over 250 pro-slavery Missouri Border Ruffians in an invasion of Kansas to destroy the Free State strongholds of Osawatomie, Lawrence, and Topeka.

On August 30, 1856, John Brown and 38 Free Staters rallied to defend Osawatomie, killing 20 Border Ruffians before they were driven off. Reid's Border Ruffians razed Osawatomie to the ground, killed five Free Staters, and took six prisoners, before raiding several more abolitionist towns, including Topeka. Kansas' acting governor, the pro-slavery Daniel Woodson, declared the territory to be in a state of rebellion, outraging the Free Staters. However, the US Army refused to get involved and on September 14, 1856, an army of 2,700 invading Border Ruffians skirmished with Brown's Free Staters outside Lawrence. Eventually, Kansas' new governor, an incredulous John W. Geary, convinced both sides to disband. Brown, now a national abolitionist hero, soon left Kansas to plan his Harpers Ferry raid. An uneasy truce largely prevailed through 1857 as the Free State settlers began to decisively win Kansas' demographic race.

However, on May 19, 1858, 30 Border Ruffians suddenly descended into Kansas. They captured 11 unarmed Free Staters and shot them execution-style, killing five, severely wounding five, and leaving one uninjured. Nevertheless, this so-called Marais des Cygnes Massacre was the last major act of political violence of the "Bleeding Kansas" period.

Kansas joins the Union, 1859–61

Kansas' 1859 elections forever ensured Republican and Free State dominance of the territory. In February 1860, the new territorial legislature finally outlawed slavery in Kansas. Meanwhile, Kansas' fourth proposed state constitution, drafted in Wyandotte, banned slavery and was approved by Kansas voters in October 1859. It was then submitted to a reluctant Congress, which pigeonholed it to avoid antagonizing the South. By late 1860, the Kansas Territory governor, George M. Beebe, would even propose that in the event of national civil war Kansas should declare neutrality and "establish, under a Constitution of her own creation, a Government to be separate and independent among the Nations." However, the overwhelming majority of Kansans supported the North and rejected independence out of hand.

Republican Abraham Lincoln won the US presidential election on November 6, 1860. In response, South Carolina became the first slave state to secede from the Union on December 20. By late January 1861, six Southern slave states had seceded, making Kansas' Free State status a moot point. On January 29, 1861, Congress approved the Wyandotte Constitution and Kansas was admitted to the Union as the 34th state. Kansas then had a population of 107,206, heavily concentrated within 60 miles of the Missouri border. The new state's capital was Topeka, a town of 800 surrounded by "howling wilderness."

Kansas' largest settlement in 1861 was Leavenworth, boasting 5,000 residents, followed by Atchison with 2,500. Leavenworth had the state's only telegraph service. Lawrence had a population of 2,000 while seven other towns reached at least 500 residents. The state's only operational railroad was a tiny, strategically irrelevant five-mile line along the Missouri River. The state's first important railroad, a 38-mile Kansas Pacific line connecting Wyandotte and Lawrence, would only become operational on November 28, 1864, a month after Westport.

Kansas' western three-quarters remained uncivilized wilderness throughout the Civil War; Federal troops stationed in Kansas were usually more concerned with defending Kansans from hostile Indians than the unlikely marauding Confederate Army.

CONFEDERATE ACTIONS IN MISSOURI, 1861–63

Missouri's central location along the Mississippi River combined with St. Louis' large size and logistical importance made Missouri a strategically important state within the wider American Civil War. Although most Missouri farmers did not own slaves, most believed free black men would represent a threat to their own economic wellbeing. Modern research nevertheless suggests Missourians favored Union over secession by a 2:1 margin. Whatever their original allegiance, years of brutal depredations by indiscriminate militants on both sides would affect individual and household loyalties throughout Missouri.

By late 1860, the outgoing Missouri governor, the Northern-sympathizing Robert Marcellus Stewart, proclaimed a policy of neutrality in case of national hostilities, which seemed increasingly likely. Missouri would not send troops or provisions to either side, and Missouri troops would fight forces from either side that entered the state. This policy of wary armed neutrality was publicly restated in early 1861 by the incoming Missouri governor, the Southern-leaning Claiborne Fox Jackson. However, Jackson was a closet secessionist and immediately began conspiring with fellow Missouri secessionists to both seize the US government arsenal at St. Louis and to illegally funnel Missouri bank money into funding pro-secession Missouri troops.

On March 19, 1861, the Missouri Constitutional Convention voted 89-to-1 against secession. However, on April 20, 1861, secessionist Missouri militia captured the Federal government's Liberty Arsenal at Liberty, Missouri, near Kansas City. On April 29, the US Army's Captain Nathaniel Lyon's Federal troops evacuated 21,000 of the St. Louis Arsenal's 39,000 guns to Illinois. Governor Jackson then ordered the Missouri State Militia (MSM) into Camp Jackson outside St. Louis ostensibly for maneuvers. Then, on May 9, Lyon discovered a secret shipment of Confederate artillery. The following day, May 10, Lyon attacked the MSM at Camp Jackson and captured it, before marching the prisoners under guard through St. Louis for internment at the St. Louis Arsenal. A riot soon erupted and nervous Federal troops, mostly German immigrants, fired into the crowd and killed 28 civilians.

The following day, the Missouri General Assembly formally established the new Missouri State Guard (MSG) under Major General Sterling Price. Ostensibly, the MSG was to repel invasions from either side; in actuality, both Jackson and Price had messaged the Confederate government to send troops into Missouri and drive out the Federal presence.

However, on May 21, 1861, Brigadier General William S. Harney, commander of the Federal Department of the West, signed the Price–Harney Truce with Sterling Price. The truce was intended to forestall miscommunication and open conflict in Missouri, but was widely unpopular throughout the Union

Frederic Edwin Church's 1861 *Our Banner in the Sky* representing patriotism to the Union after the Confederate attack on Fort Sumter that April inaugurated the American Civil War. Both North and South believed a short victory was at hand and both proved badly mistaken. (Frederic Edwin Church, public domain, via Wikimedia Commons)

for its supposed leniency. On May 30, President Abraham Lincoln replaced Harney with the firebrand Lyon, effectively ending the truce.

Open fighting soon broke out. On June 17, 1861, at Boonville, Missouri, a Federal force of 1,600 troops defeated an MSG force of 500 men. The Federal victory at Boonville helped establish eventual full Federal control of the Missouri River, which dominated the state, as well as keeping subjugated Little Dixie, the state's most ardently pro-slavery region.

The Confederates nevertheless still dominated southwest Missouri. On July 5, 1861 an MSG force of 6,000 men and seven guns defeated a Federal force of 1,100 men and eight guns at Carthage, forcing the Federals to fall back 60 miles to Springfield.

The Federal situation in southwest Missouri continued to deteriorate. On August 10, 1861, Brigadier General Lyon's outnumbered Federal force of 5,431 troops attacked a combined force of 12,125 Confederates and pro-Confederate MSG troops under Major General Sterling Price at Wilson's Creek. By noon, Lyon had been killed and the surviving Federals withdrew back to Springfield, ten miles to the southwest. Wilson's Creek was the first major battle of the war fought west of the Mississippi and gave the Confederates control of southwestern Missouri.

In central Missouri, Colonel William Breckenridge Brown's 800 MSG men attacked 140 Unionist militia at Boonville on September 13, 1861. The Boonville Unionists repulsed the MSG force and killed Colonel Brown.

Missouri seemingly remained up for grabs. A week later, on September 20, Price's own MSG force captured the 3,500-man garrison at Lexington, Missouri, along with 3,000 small arms, 750 horses, and $100,000 worth of provisions. But Price was soon compelled to withdraw, first from Lexington, and then from Missouri entirely over the coming months.

Meanwhile, in the fall of 1861, Missouri Governor Claiborne Jackson and other prominent Missouri secessionists convened at Neosho, Missouri, and proclaimed themselves the Missouri General Assembly. On October 28, 1861, this dubious legislature passed an ordinance of secession. However, the proclamation was largely ignored by Missouri Unionists, who made up most of the state. Nevertheless, the Confederate States of America officially accepted Jackson's secessionist shadow government and, on November 28, proclaimed Missouri the Confederacy's 12th state. Like Kansas a few years earlier, Missouri now had two dueling governments.

A contemporary illustration of the March 7–8, 1862 battle of Pea Ridge, Arkansas, as imagined by the journal *Harper's Weekly*. Pea Ridge was arguably Curtis' finest hour prior to the Westport campaign and although it took place in northwest Arkansas, it signaled the end of realistic Confederate control over the neighboring state of Missouri. (Missouri Historical Society, public domain, via Wikimedia Commons)

On December 25, 1861, Brigadier General Samuel Curtis assumed command of the Federal Army of the Southwest. By early 1862, Curtis had pushed Price's MSG entirely out of Missouri and into Arkansas. Governor Jackson's Confederate shadow government was also driven out of Missouri entirely in 1862. It would be forced to seat its capital in Marshall, Texas, through to the end of the war. Governor Jackson died of cancer and in late 1862 would be replaced as Confederate governor by Thomas Reynolds.

On March 7–8, 1862, Curtis' 10,250-man Army of the Southwest defeated Major General Earl Van Dorn's 16,500-strong Army of the West at Pea Ridge in northwest Arkansas, essentially denying the Confederacy formal control of Missouri. Both the Federal and Confederate governments now began drawing forces out of the Missouri–Arkansas theater and transferring them east. These included Price's MSG, which was formally incorporated into the Confederate Army.

Price's finest cavalry general, the dashing and chivalrous Joseph "Jo" Shelby. On July 4, 1865, Shelby and 200 defiant officers and men of the Missouri Brigade would reach the Rio Grande. Here Shelby and his men weighed down their Confederate battle flags with stones and sank them into the river before crossing into Mexico and Southern immortality as the "undefeated" Confederates. (Public domain)

Despite the drawdown of regular forces, throughout 1862, the loyalty of Missouri's home front remained up for grabs, with Unionist militias and Confederate recruiters clashing for statewide control. In August 1862, pro-Southern forces nearly attained control of northwest Missouri's Jackson County (Kansas City) at the battles of Independence and Lone Jack. On August 6, 1862, Colonel John McNeil's 2nd Missouri Cavalry of 1,000 men defeated a Confederate brigade of 2,000 recruits at Kirksville, securing Federal control of northeast Missouri.

However, a Confederate force of 5,000 defeated 4,000 Federals at Newtonia on September 30, 1862. A second Confederate victory at Clark's Mill on November 7 threatened Federal control of southwest Missouri, inspiring Confederate Major General Thomas Hindman to conduct raids into the state from Arkansas. Missourian Brigadier General John Marmaduke would lead two unsuccessful Confederate raids aimed at southern Missouri in January and April 1863. However, Marmaduke's former subordinate, Colonel Joseph "Jo" Shelby, was more successful that summer. Between August 21 and November 3, 1863, Shelby, one of the Confederacy's finest cavalry commanders and, like Marmaduke, a future division commander at Westport, led a daring cavalry raid through northwest Arkansas and western Missouri. Shelby's Raid would inflict considerable damage, but cost about 150 casualties. Upon his return, Shelby was promoted to brigadier general. Nevertheless, the basic strategic situation in Missouri remained unchanged.

THE KANSAS–MISSOURI BORDER WAR, 1861–64

The outbreak of open war in 1861 allowed those with long-simmering resentments within Kansas and Missouri the political excuse to resume the Bleeding Kansas fighting. However, this new conflict, eventually called the Border War, would far exceed Bleeding Kansas in scale, complexity, and

Kansas Senator James H. "Jim" Lane – the "Grim Chieftain" and prominent Jayhawker – was born in Indiana and was 50 years old during the Westport campaign. Lane was a darkly charismatic, mercurial man of no true convictions. Full details of his incredibly colorful life are impossible to fit here, but Lane would serve as a Curtis staff member at Westport before committing suicide after the war. (kansasmemory.org, Kansas State Historical Society)

violence. Between 1861 and 1864, Kansans and Missourians would both inflict and suffer mass terrorism, piracy, irregular warfare, counter-insurgency operations, and mass civilian relocation – all committed by Americans against Americans in America. This situation is possibly unique in the nation's history. Indeed the entire Kansas–Missouri Border War comprised a messy juxtaposition of nation-state politics, regular armies, ideological radicals, irregular vigilantes, external invasions, native guerrilla warfare, and widespread, indiscriminate civilian suffering.

Realistically, the Border War chaos and lawlessness gave society's latent sociopaths and psychopaths on both sides their opening to rape, plunder, and commit mass murder, all while claiming a thin veneer of justification by pretending to adopt radical moral ideologies they perhaps cared little about.

On the Kansas side, many adventurous Kansans proudly claimed the dubious and murky mantle of "Jayhawkers" – a title adopted both by completely lawless criminals as well as fully legal Kansas volunteer cavalry regiments of the US Army. Many prominent Jayhawkers slipped back and forth between the types during their wartime careers. The Jayhawkers' goal was typically to raid Missouri, often regardless of their targets' national loyalty, although the formal volunteer regiments were still expected to somewhat follow official orders.

An 1896 history described Jayhawkers thus: "Confederated at first for defense against pro-slavery outrages, but ultimately falling more or less completely into the vocation of robbers and assassins, they have received the name – whatever its origins may be – of Jayhawkers."

The Jayhawkers also incorporated a bizarre streak of radical progressivism within their otherwise lawless ranks, often including freed black slaves within their bands. Nevertheless, many Jayhawkers were virtually terrorists whose morality and military accomplishments were often dubious.

By late June 1861, radical Kansas Jayhawker chieftains Colonel James Montgomery and Lieutenant Colonel Charles "Doc" Jennison, not content with static border defense, began raiding western Missouri, plundering farms and freeing and arming slaves, Montgomery explaining that the best way "to keep the Missourians from our doors was to give them something to do at home."

In August 1861, Kansas' radical, fiery, and darkly charismatic but psychologically unstable US Senator Jim Lane arrived in Fort Scott, Kansas, claiming a bogus brigadier general commission. After commandeering the undisciplined 3rd, 4th, and 5th Kansas Volunteer regiments, Lane led his new "Kansas brigade" of virtually lawless Jayhawkers into Missouri ostensibly on a military patrol but actually to plunder. On September 23, 1861, Lane's Jayhawkers sacked the town of Osceola. Lane summarily executed nine Osceola men after a drumhead court-martial, freed 200 local slaves, stole 350 horses, 400 cattle, 3,000 bags of flour, numerous carriages and wagons, and finally burned Osceola to the ground in one of the Jayhawkers' most notorious wartime episodes.

Within weeks, a former Missouri State Guardsman named William C. Quantrill was raising his own band of pro-Confederate Missouri guerrillas known as Quantrill's Raiders. These were among the first of the so-called

Missouri bushwhackers, the pro-Confederate counterparts to the Jayhawkers.

With its dueling bands of vigilante guerrillas, the Kansas–Missouri theater quickly devolved into a chaotic nightmare of sudden and random mass violence and banditry, usually inflicted against civilians. Historian Charles D. Collins observed, "For many the war was only an excuse to settle old grudges."

According to the Union's Major General Henry Halleck, then general-in-chief of all Federal armies: "The conduct of the forces under Lane and Jennison has done more for the enemy in this State [Missouri] than could have been accomplished by 20,000 of his own army. I receive almost daily complaints of outrages committed by these men in the name of the United States."

By early 1862, the new Confederate commander in Arkansas, Major General Thomas Hindman, vowed to take the war back into Missouri by recruiting additional guerrilla partisans for the Confederate cause.

Halleck responded on March 13, 1862, with General Order No. 2, which claimed that guerrillas were not formal soldiers but outlaws. Pro-Confederate guerrillas, such as the Missouri bushwhackers, would therefore be summarily executed if captured. With nothing to lose, the bushwhackers simply adopted the "no quarter" policy for themselves.

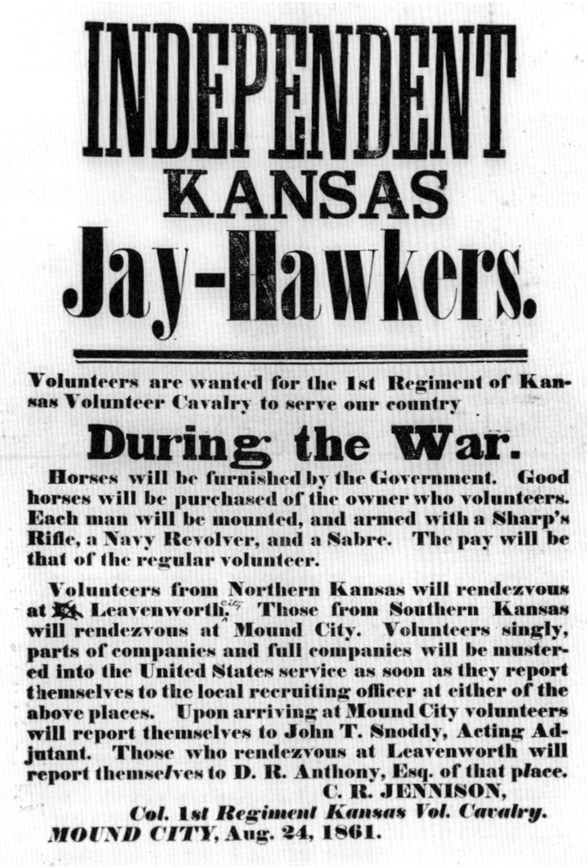
INDEPENDENT
KANSAS
Jay-Hawkers.

Volunteers are wanted for the 1st Regiment of Kansas Volunteer Cavalry to serve our country

During the War.

Horses will be furnished by the Government. Good horses will be purchased of the owner who volunteers. Each man will be mounted, and armed with a Sharp's Rifle, a Navy Revolver, and a Sabre. The pay will be that of the regular volunteer.

Volunteers from Northern Kansas will rendezvous at Leavenworth. Those from Southern Kansas will rendezvous at Mound City. Volunteers singly, parts of companies and full companies will be mustered into the United States service as soon as they report themselves to the local recruiting officer at either of the above places. Upon arriving at Mound City volunteers will report themselves to John T. Snoddy, Acting Adjutant. Those who rendezvous at Leavenworth will report themselves to D. R. Anthony, Esq. of that place.

C. R. JENNISON,

Col. 1st Regiment Kansas Vol. Cavalry.

MOUND CITY, Aug. 24, 1861.

A flyer recruiting Kansans to Charles "Doc" Jennison's 1st Kansas Volunteer Cavalry based out of Mound City. These were the original Jayhawkers of Civil War infamy, who became known for their lawlessness as much as their anti-slavery fanaticism. (Kansas Historical Society, public domain, via Wikimedia Commons)

The Confederate government countered in April 1862 with the Partisan Ranger Act, claiming bushwhackers were formal members of the Confederate Army, but this proclamation was ignored both by the Union and the bushwhackers themselves, who refused to be controlled by a higher authority.

Throughout 1862 and 1863, Jayhawkers continued to raid Missouri and bushwhackers continued to raid both Kansas and Missouri, although in both cases Federal authorities did their best to get the situation under control. In the case of the nominally Unionist Jayhawkers, the worst leaders or units could be punished or transferred east to a different theater entirely, but the bushwhackers were a different story.

Between March and November 1862, the most prominent bushwhacker band, Quantrill's Raiders, would sack the Kansas towns of Aubry, Olathe, and Shawnee Town, as well as Lamar, Missouri, murdering dozens of civilians.

On August 21, 1863, Quantrill's 450 Missouri bushwhackers descended onto the Kansas abolitionist bastion of Lawrence, murdering 150 men and boys and burning much of the city. Quantrill's principal target, Jim Lane, escaped death by fleeing to a ravine in his nightshirt. The Lawrence Massacre was the single largest civilian mass murder of the war. The atrocity shocked the entire Union and enraged the Kansas public, threatening to spiral the Border War completely out of control.

The August 21, 1863 sacking of Lawrence by William Quantrill and about 450 of his bushwhackers as portrayed in this illustration by *Harper's Weekly*. The incident shocked the nation at large and remains a defining historical event to the Lawrence community to this day. (Library of Congress, Prints and Photographs Division)

In response, Brigadier General Thomas J. Ewing, commander of the Federal District of the Border, issued the infamous General Order No. 11 on August 25, 1863. General Order No. 11 required the complete depopulation of Missouri's Bates, Cass, Jackson, and Vernon counties on the Kansas border, which Federal officials believed provided friendly staging areas for Missouri bushwhackers. Ewing then razed the empty homes and the four counties quickly became known as the "Burnt District."

Ewing intended General Order No. 11 not only to stamp out pro-Confederate bushwhacker activity, but to discourage pro-Union vigilante activity by the Jayhawkers. Indeed, on September 9, 1863, Lane gathered 1,000 Jayhawkers at Paola, Kansas, and marched towards Westport, Missouri, to burn it down, only backing down when confronted by several

General Order No. 11 as depicted by George Caleb Bingham in 1863. Although Bingham was a Union supporter, his propagandistic painting sympathizes with a slave-holding family seeing its farm burned and son shot. The Federal officer is visibly wearing "red legs", made infamous by a particular Jayhawker band. (Historic Collection/Alamy Stock Photo)

11th Kansas Calvary companies Ewing had sent to stop them.

Meanwhile, by late 1863, Quantrill's 400 bushwhackers were heading south through Kansas to overwinter in Texas. En route, Quantrill decided to attack southeast Kansas' Fort Baxter. On October 6, 1863, Quantrill's column attacked the fort and was repulsed by 25 cavalry and 75 men of the 2nd Kansas Colored Infantry. Hours later, Quantrill discovered and ambushed a Federal column of 175 cavalry escorting Major General James G. Blunt to his new assignment. Quantrill's men killed 103 Federal troops, including many attempting to surrender. Among the few escaping survivors was Blunt himself.

Quantrill's Raider's battle flag. The Confederate Partisan Ranger Act of 1862 authorized any group of ten men to organize and elect a captain, sergeant, and corporal to fight against Federal forces. In this respect the Partisan Ranger Act resembled traditional letters of marque authorizing naval privateer operations. (Kansas Historical Society, public domain, via Wikimedia Commons)

THE STRATEGIC SITUATION, 1864

While Kansas and Missouri descended into virtual frontier anarchy, the American Civil War as a whole played out on a much larger and more decisive national stage back East. Although unclear at the time, the twin Federal victories at Gettysburg, Pennsylvania, and Vicksburg, Mississippi, on July 3–4, 1863, had effectively ended the Confederacy's window of winning independence through outright military victory. However, final Union victory remained uncertain. As 1864 dawned, there was no clear end to the war in sight. Confederate morale remained high and the Union home front suffered from a pronounced war-weariness. A Confederate political victory was still possible, as the Union was scheduled for national elections in November 1864.

Looking to unseat Republican Abraham Lincoln as president was Lincoln's former general-in-chief, George B. McClellan. Although privately pro-war, McClellan represented the anti-war wing of the Democratic Party (whom the Republicans derisively nicknamed "Copperheads" for their allegedly treacherous nature). As an ardent Unionist, Lincoln's entire presidency had been consumed by the singular issue of crushing the Southern insurrection. This inevitably made the 1864 presidential election a Northern referendum on whether to continue prosecuting the war. The Union's precarious political situation was well recognized on both sides. The result was that both Confederate and Federal military strategies during 1864 were heavily intended to influence the Union's November 1864 elections.

In March 1864, President Lincoln promoted Ulysses S. Grant to lieutenant general and awarded Grant field command of all Union armies. Lincoln would have it no other way; when challenged on Grant's qualifications, Lincoln responded, "I cannot spare this man. He fights." In addition to praising Grant's aggressiveness and proven success in the field, Lincoln wholeheartedly agreed with Grant's strategy to win the war against the South.

The strategic situation, 1864

Grant would exploit superior Union strength and logistics by striking in a coordinated manner at the Confederacy's heart from all directions. From now on, constant pressure would be maintained and retreats would be forbidden. In accordance with Grant's new strategy, between March 10 and June 9, 1864, the Union launched four separate, major strategic offensives against the Confederacy, reflecting growing Federal military power.

Major General George Meade's Army of the Potomac and Major General Benjamin Butler's Army of the James would combine to press Confederate General Robert E. Lee's Army of Northern Virginia in the Richmond area, while Major General Franz Sigel would invade Virginia's fertile Shenandoah Valley to starve Lee out. Grant's former lieutenant, Major General William T. Sherman, would lead Grant's old Army of the Tennessee in an invasion of Georgia against Confederate General Joseph E. Johnston's Army of Tennessee. Finally, Major General Nathaniel Banks would lead a Federal army to capture East Texas and Shreveport, Louisiana, securing control over Louisiana's Red River. Although Banks' Red River campaign quickly failed, the remaining three Federal offensives would ultimately succeed.

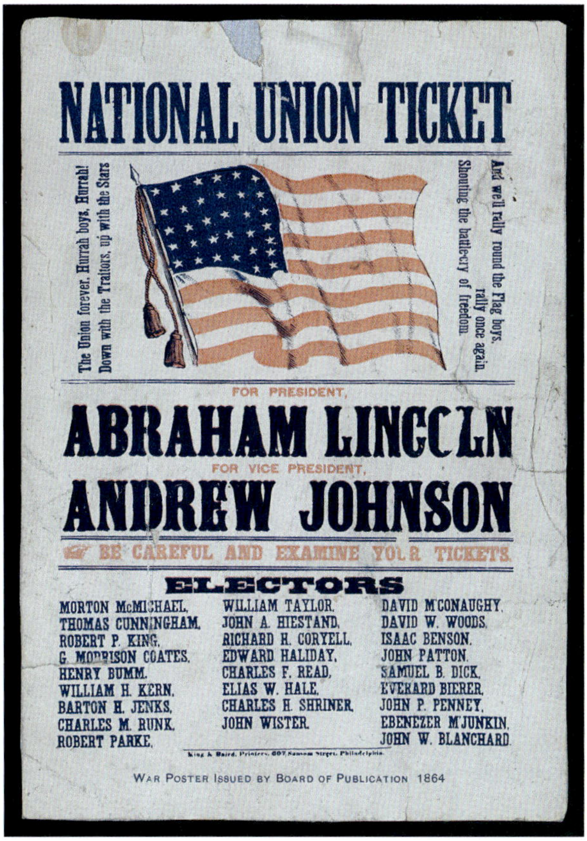

An 1864 poster proclaiming the Lincoln–Johnson presidential ticket. For political purposes, Lincoln chose a fervently pro-Union Southern Democrat, Andrew Johnson, as his running mate. Likewise the Republican Party and the pro-war Democrats temporarily joined forces as the "National Union" party and were opposed by peace-seeking Democrats called Copperheads. (Library of Congress, Rare Book and Special Collections Division, Alfred Whital Stern Collection of Lincolniana)

Indeed, by August 1864, the Federal Army had captured four of the Confederacy's 11 state capitals; another two, Richmond and Atlanta, were under siege by Meade's and Sherman's armies, respectively. On September 2, Sherman would capture Atlanta. This was a key turning point in Northern public opinion, and seemed to assure both Lincoln's re-election in November and an inevitable final victory over the Confederacy.

Meanwhile, back on July 21, 1864, the Confederate General Braxton Bragg had been in Columbus, Georgia, analyzing Lieutenant General John Bell Hood's defeat to Sherman the previous day. Suddenly realizing the extreme danger the Confederacy faced, Bragg appears to have panicked. He fired off a message to Lieutenant General Stephen D. Lee, the temporary commander of the Confederacy's Department of Alabama and Mississippi, stating, "The President orders a prompt movement of Lieutenant General Taylor and the infantry of his corps to cross the Mississippi." In fact, Confederate president Jefferson Davis later claimed to have no record of the alleged order. Nevertheless, by July 23, Lieutenant General Lee had wired the supposed order to General E. Kirby Smith, Taylor's superior and commander of the Trans-Mississippi Department.

In fact, the order to cross the Mississippi was nearly dead on arrival. The most immediate reason was because the Mississippi River itself was under the total control of US Navy gunboats. However, Smith amended this to a plan "to push a large cavalry force into Missouri and support the [Arkansas] movement." For political reasons, Smith was forced to put

LEFT
Lieutenant General Ulysses S. Grant seen in a photograph during the 1864 Overland Campaign. Grant was the architect of the overall Union strategy to win the war in the East by leaving the Trans-Mississippi Theater thinly defended. (Library of Congress, public domain, via Wikimedia Commons)

RIGHT
Confederate General Edmund Kirby Smith commanded the Confederate Trans-Mississippi Department. Smith's department was so isolated from the Confederate government at large that it was referred to as "Kirby Smithdom" and Confederate president Jefferson Davis genuinely believed Smith might secede his department from the Confederacy entirely. (Civil War photographs, 1861–1865, Library of Congress, Prints and Photographs Division)

the Missourian Major General Sterling Price in command of the planned Missouri Expedition, which Smith ordered on August 4, 1864.

Although largely remembered as "Price's Raid," the Confederates' September–October 1864 Missouri campaign was considerably larger and slower than a raid, and its objectives were to take and hold cities and territory long enough to hold elections. This is more accurately a persistence strategy rather than a raid, and recent historians have begun referring to Price's campaign as the Missouri Expedition.

CHRONOLOGY

1860

November 6	Abraham Lincoln elected president of the United States.
December 20	South Carolina becomes the first state to secede from the Union.

1861

January 29	The US Congress admits Kansas as a State of the Union.
March 19	Missouri legislature votes to remain in the Union.
April 12	Confederacy fires on Fort Sumter, beginning the American Civil War.
April 17	Missouri's Governor Jackson refuses to comply with Lincoln's April 15 proclamation to call up Federal volunteers.
April 20	Pro-Southern militia seize US arsenal at Liberty, Missouri.
May 4	Pro-Southern militia seize US ordnance at Kansas City, Missouri.
May 10	Federal Captain Lyon captures pro-Southern militia forces at Camp Jackson, Missouri, prompting a civilian mob to attack Federal troops at St. Louis.
June 14	Federal troops secure Kansas City.
June 15	Lyon's Federal soldiers seize Missouri State Capitol at Jefferson City.
June 17	First battle of Boonville.
August 10	Battle of Wilson's Creek.
September 23	Lane's Jayhawker brigade sacks Osceola, Missouri.
October 28	Deposed Missouri secessionists pass Ordinance of Secession in Neosho.
November 28	Confederacy officially admits secessionist Missouri shadow government.

1862

March 7–8	Battle of Pea Ridge, Arkansas gives Federals initiative in Missouri.
December 7	Battle of Prairie Grove assures Federal control of northwest Arkansas.

1863

August 21	Quantrill's band of 450 bushwhackers raids Lawrence, Kansas, killing at least 150 civilians.

August 21–November 3	Shelby's Raid through Missouri.
August 25	Federals' General Order No. 11 forces the expulsion of all residents in the Missouri border region of Jackson, Cass, Bates, and Vernon counties.
October 6	Baxter Springs Massacre.

1864

March–May	Federals' Red River campaign in northern Louisiana fails.
August 4	Smith orders Price to invade Missouri.
August 28	Price departs Camden, Arkansas, on Missouri Expedition.
September 7	Price crosses Arkansas River at Dardanelle.
September 14	Price and the Marmaduke and Fagan Divisions arrive in Pocahontas, Arkansas.
September 17	Shelby's Division joins Price's Army of Missouri at Pocahontas.
September 19	Price's army enters Missouri.
September 27	Centralia Massacre.
September 27–28	Battle of Fort Davidson.
October 1	Price abandons planned move against St. Louis.
October 7–8	Price arrives at Jefferson City, then abandons assault.
October 9	Governor Carney calls up Kansas militia to defend against Confederate invasion.
October 10	Curtis declares martial law in Kansas.
October 10–12	Price rests Army of Missouri at Boonville.
October 13	Curtis designates his newly established Kansas field force as the Army of the Border.
October 15	Battles of Glasgow and Sedalia.
October 19	Battle of Lexington.
October 21	Battles of Independence and the Little Blue River.
October 22–23	Battle of Westport.
October 22	Battles of Independence and Byram's Ford (Big Blue River) just outside Kansas City (battle of Westport).

October 23	Federals decisively defeat Price at the battles of Brush Creek and Byram's Ford, ensuring victory at the battle of Westport. Price retreats south along Kansas–Missouri border.
October 24	Pursuing Federals close gap with Price's surviving army.
October 25	Federals overtake Price's rearguard and force three cavalry battles along the Kansas–Missouri border, climaxing at Mine Creek.
October 26	Bloody Bill Anderson killed in Albany, Missouri, in an ambush.
October 28	Battle of Newtonia.
November 8	Abraham Lincoln wins re-election as US president. Kansas Governor Carney loses re-election to Samuel J. Crawford. Curtis ends pursuit of Price at the Arkansas River.
December 2	After detouring through Indian Territory and Texas, Price arrives back in Arkansas, largely ending the Civil War in Kansas and Missouri.

OPPOSING COMMANDERS

CONFEDERATE

The Confederate War Department's General Order No. 39 established the Trans-Mississippi Department on May 26, 1862. The Trans-Mississippi was a territorial department encompassing Missouri, Arkansas, Texas, Indian Territory (modern-day Oklahoma), Arizona Territory, and Louisiana west of the Mississippi River.

By 1864, the Trans-Mississippi was commanded by **General Edmund Kirby Smith** from his headquarters in Shreveport, Louisiana. The fall of Vicksburg in July 1863 cut the Trans-Mississippi off from the eastern Confederacy. Smith's command was now practically autonomous and nicknamed "Kirby Smithdom." In 1863, Confederate president Jefferson Davis sent a letter to Smith addressing rumors that the Trans-Mississippi might secede from the Confederacy. Smith would surrender his army at Galveston, Texas, on June 2, 1865, the last major surrender of a Confederate force in the field.

Governor Thomas C. Reynolds was the head of the Confederate Missouri shadow government meeting in exile at Marshall, Texas. Reynolds accompanied the Price expedition, but his dislike of Price grew throughout the campaign. Reynolds fled to Mexico after the Confederacy's defeat, but returned to Missouri in 1869, where he committed suicide 20 years later.

Major General Sterling Price commanded the Army of Missouri. The 55-year-old Price, a wealthy plantation owner from Missouri's Little Dixie region, was a popular, longtime Missouri politician and soldier, having served in the Mexican War and as governor of Missouri between 1853 and 1857. Price was appointed commander of the newly established pro-Confederate MSG in May 1861 and won a major victory at Wilson's Creek, Missouri, three months later, but his star was dashed by his subsequent 1862 defeat at Pea Ridge, Arkansas.

Price apparently inspired highly charged opinions; he was often described as being a noble man of high character, yet Confederate Missouri Governor Reynolds found Price "devious, insincere, petulant, and arrogant," while General Kirby Smith also much despised Price in character and military skill. Tall and aristocratic, Price had been regal and handsome in 1861, but by 1864 he weighed 300lb and rode a mule-driven carriage because he could no longer mount a horse.

Nicknamed "Old Pap," Price was a career infantry commander and he led his cavalry raid like an infantryman. Price was named the leader of the 1864 Missouri Expedition not by talent or popularity but by political default. Price would survive the war but died in St. Louis in 1867.

LEFT
Arkansan Major General James F. Fagan was the only non-Missourian major general of Price's expedition. Fagan fought in the Mexican War and on April 25, 1864, his brigade helped destroy a Federal supply train at the battle of Marks' Mills in southern Arkansas. (National Portrait Gallery, public domain, via Wikimedia Commons)

RIGHT
Major General John S. Marmaduke was born in Saline County, Missouri, on March 14, 1833. Like Price, he owned a slave plantation in Missouri's Little Dixie region along the Missouri River. In 1884 Marmaduke would be elected governor of Missouri partly by exploiting his Confederate history and romanticizing Confederate and bushwhacker exploits in the state. Marmaduke would die in office in 1887. (PMAF Collection/ Alamy Stock Photo)

Price's Army of Missouri comprised three mounted divisions, each consisting of two to four brigades. Per Confederate practice, divisions and brigades were named after their commanders.

Major General James F. Fagan was the 36-year-old commander of Fagan's Division. An Arkansan, Fagan was the only non-Missourian of the four army and division commanders. Fagan participated in the early 1864 Camden Expedition, before being assigned to the Missouri Expedition.

Major General John S. Marmaduke, a 31-year-old Missourian and 1857 West Point graduate, commanded the Marmaduke Division. Marmaduke had resigned from the MSG after his June 17, 1861 rout at Boonville and was commissioned into the Confederate Army.

Marmaduke's morality was dubious. In September 1863, Marmaduke killed a Confederate brigadier general in a duel. Then at Poison Spring, Arkansas, on April 18, 1864, Marmaduke's soldiers massacred 117 members of the 1st Kansas Colored Volunteers, many after surrendering. Marmaduke would become governor of Missouri in 1885 and die in office two years later.

The dashing 33-year-old **Brigadier General Joseph O. Shelby** commanded the Shelby Division. In 1863, Colonel Shelby established his own Arkansas-based cavalry brigade, later nicknamed the "Iron Brigade." Shelby later led the brigade in the August–November 1863 raid through Arkansas and Missouri.

As the most skilled cavalry general in Price's army, Shelby was always given the most difficult and critical jobs by Price. Whenever Price was defeated in the field, it was usually Shelby's men making the Army of Missouri's valiant last stand. Shelby never surrendered after the Civil War, fleeing to Mexico and service in the Mexican Army.

Missouri bushwhackers also participated in Price's Raid. The most prominent band was Quantrill's Raiders, which had formed in 1862 around the moody and mercurial **Captain William C. Quantrill.** Although capable of decisive action, by late 1864, Quantrill had been eclipsed by his former subordinate **William "Bloody Bill" Anderson**, a 24-year-old genuine psychopath who reveled in torture and murder. The notoriously brutal Anderson was nevertheless a brilliant guerrilla fighter. A third prominent

A portrait of William C. Quantrill. Quantrill received an official officer's commission from the Confederate government, but, like other guerrillas, operated outside any real semblance of Confederate authority. Ironically, Quantrill had once been a Lawrence, Kansas, schoolteacher. (B. James George, Sr. Photograph Collection, State Historical Society of Missouri, public domain)

bushwhacker leader was **Lieutenant George Todd**, who like Anderson had been a Quantrill disciple. Todd was noteworthy in reprimanding Anderson for the Centralia Massacre. Todd would be shot and killed near the Little Blue River on October 22, 1864.

FEDERAL

Kansas and Missouri were backwaters; the Federal government did not expect anything decisive in this theater. Furthermore, by mid-1864, the widespread guerrilla warfare that had typified the region had fallen off dramatically, and both Kansas and Missouri had become convenient casting-off places for Federal generals who had fallen out of favor in Washington.

The US War Department divided the United States into geographically based departments. The Department of Missouri had been established on November 9, 1861. After several reorganizations, by July 1864, it comprised the state of Missouri alone and was divided into five districts – Northwest Missouri, Central Missouri, St. Louis, Rolla, and Southwest Missouri. When on campaign each district commander would command a field force, usually a brigade of cavalry.

Major General William S. Rosecrans commanded the full Department of Missouri. Nicknamed "Old Rosy," Rosecrans was a devout Catholic wielding an extraordinary temper. After the disastrous battle of Chickamauga, Rosecrans was removed from command of the Army of the Cumberland in October 1863. After several months of career purgatory, in January 1864 Rosecrans was essentially "kicked downstairs" to the Missouri theater.

In October 1864, **Major General Alfred S. Pleasonton** would form and command the Department of Missouri's Provisional Cavalry Division of four separate brigades. A career dragoon/cavalryman, Pleasonton had been promoted to major general and commander of the Federal Cavalry Corps in June 1863 before Grant personally replaced Pleasonton with Sheridan.

By early 1864, Pleasonton had been placed on leave in Pennsylvania, pending his transfer to the backwater Department of Missouri. However, Price's invasion of Missouri prompted Rosecrans to recall Pleasonton, who arrived in St. Louis on October 6. Despite Pleasonton's mixed reputation as a wartime officer, he performed well at Westport and the subsequent pursuit of Price that climaxed at Mine Creek.

Brigadier General Thomas J. Ewing, Jr. commanded the Department of Missouri's District of St. Louis, which was further divided into three sub-districts. Ewing led the defense of Fort Davidson at Pilot Knob.

Major General Andrew Jackson (A.J.) Smith commanded the XVI Corps, a provisional formation independent of the Department of Missouri but called on to help chase Price across Missouri. After his infantry were force-marched across Missouri in miserable weather, Smith's superiors' poor decision-making would rob Smith of a golden opportunity to destroy a Confederate army in the field.

The US War Department had re-established the Department of Kansas on January 1, 1864. By the time of the Westport campaign, the Department of Kansas comprised the state of Kansas and the neighboring territories of Nebraska and Colorado. The department was divided into five districts: North

LEFT
Major General William S. Rosecrans, or "Old Rosy," had achieved early fame winning the 1862 battles of Iuka and Corinth while under the command of Grant. However, Rosecrans' brusque, outspoken nature won him few friends and after the disastrous defeat at Chickamauga in 1863 Rosecrans was transferred west to the Department of Missouri. (Library of Congress, public domain, via Wikimedia Commons)

RIGHT
Major General Samuel Curtis had been in command at the Union's March 1862 victory at Pea Ridge, Arkansas. By June 12, Curtis had captured Helena, Arkansas, on the Mississippi River. By 1863, Curtis would be assigned to command Union troops in Kansas, as his abolitionist views made him an impractical choice for command in Missouri. (Library of Congress, public domain, via Wikimedia Commons)

Kansas, South Kansas, Upper Arkansas (western Kansas), and the Territories of Colorado and Nebraska.

Governor Thomas Carney was the moderate Republican governor of Kansas and political arch-enemy of Senator Jim Lane, the Radical Republican demagogue and chief Jayhawker of them all. Carney proved late in calling up the Kansas militia, as he initially believed the Price expedition was a Radical Republican conspiracy to interfere with the upcoming state elections.

Major General Samuel R. Curtis commanded the full Department of Kansas as well as the Army of the Border upon its formation. The 59-year-old Curtis was an 1831 West Point graduate and an engineer and lawyer by trade. A native New Yorker, Curtis had served in the Mexican–American War as the commanding colonel of the 3rd Ohio, and supervised the occupation of several Mexican cities. Like many Kansas generals, Curtis was a highly political Radical Republican of the Lane faction; however, despite Carney's anxieties, Curtis always kept his politics out of his conduct of military affairs. Curtis was additionally an excellent administrator and a capable, albeit conservative, field commander.

Major General James G. Blunt commanded Curtis' Provisional Cavalry Division of the Army of the Border. A lawyer, Radical Republican, and former Maine seaman, Blunt had both badly lost and barely survived the disastrous October 6, 1863 battle of Baxter Springs. Among those massacred under Blunt at Baxter Springs was Curtis' son Zarah; unsurprisingly, many had publicly accused Blunt of dereliction and cowardice (although not Curtis, interestingly). The moody Blunt was a hard drinker and shameless womanizer, but also a "dark and dangerous man" capable of relentless aggressiveness in the face of superior enemy forces; indeed Blunt displayed steely fortitude throughout the Westport campaign. Always psychologically unstable, Blunt was committed to a mental asylum in 1879, where he died in 1881.

A native Pennsylvanian, 38-year-old **Major General George W. Deitzler** had moved to Kansas in 1855 and become a staunch Free Stater. Deitzler raised the 1st Kansas Volunteer in 1861 and commanded a volunteer brigade at Vicksburg before resigning in August 1863 and returning to Kansas. Deitzler was then shortly appointed Kansas adjutant general and commander of the Kansas State Militia (KSM).

OPPOSING FORCES

CONFEDERATE

Price's Army of Missouri comprised three undersized cavalry divisions, totaling approximately 13,000 men, 14 light-caliber artillery pieces, and a large wagon train of supplies. Despite adding thousands of Missouri recruits en route, by the October 22–23 battle of Westport, casualties and desertions would whittle Price's army down to 8,500 men.

The Army of Missouri was organized into three divisions. Fagan's Division of Arkansans was Price's largest, with four brigades and four guns. Marmaduke's Division of Missourians comprised two Missouri brigades and five guns in two batteries, one from Missouri and one from Texas. Shelby's Division consisted of three Missouri brigades, including one of unarmed, unorganized recruits, and contained two Missouri batteries of five guns.

By late 1864, most Confederate troops lacked government-issued uniforms and wore everyday clothing. Thousands of Price's men marched without shoes, and many were or had recently been diseased from long postings in Louisiana and Arkansas swamps. About one-quarter of Price's men were untrained conscripts drafted into Confederate service, and often lacked basic issue military equipment entirely. Additionally, the proud western troops of the Trans-Mississippi held scant national loyalty to the Confederacy at large. They had not been paid in a year, were deserting in increasing numbers, and were concerned only with defending their own region. As rugged individualists, they were interested only in fighting for their homes and held no desire to fight Richmond's war.

Samuel J. Reader's depiction of Confederate cavalry at Westport. By 1864, the Confederate cavalry arm was suffering heavily from lack of proper mounts, with many of Price's men riding mules or being dismounted entirely during the Missouri Expedition. (kansasmemory.org, Kansas State Historical Society)

Confederate cavalry

The Confederate cavalry had once been the finest combat arm on either side, but by late 1864, it was a shadow of its former self. A major reason for this was that the best warhorses were long gone; a Confederate cavalryman was expected to provide his own horse and there was never any state-funded cavalry horse breeding system in the

Confederacy as there was in the Union. In fact, so scarce were horses that thousands of Price's men rode mules and many hundreds had no mounts at all.

Price was additionally handicapped by his meager artillery. Confederate artillery by this point was relatively poor, despite having captured many Federal guns and horses during the 1864 Red River campaign.

After Pilot Knob, St. Louis, and finally Jefferson City, Price appears to have been insecure about his chances of ultimate success and his reputation within the Trans-Mississippi Department. The astonishing amount of plunder and wagons Price increasingly acquired and carried along with the Army of Missouri – to the great detriment of his tactical and operational speed – may have been Price's attempt to bring hard evidence of the "success" of his raid back to his superiors.

Missouri State Guard

Price's three divisions were fleshed out by MSG units. The MSG was a pro-Confederate militia, sometimes serving under Confederate officers, but not officially a part of the Confederate Army. Established by the Missouri General Assembly on May 11, 1861, the MSG was intended to defend Missouri against Federal invasion. Its strength had peaked in September 1861 at 25,000 men.

Missouri bushwhackers

Americans had a long tradition of hit-and-run irregular warfare, inspired by the typically American anti-authoritarian streak and further exacerbated by the rugged, individualist frontier culture of states such as Missouri and Kansas.

Bushwhackers were typically in their late teens or early twenties and illiterate. Many were former Border Ruffians from the Bleeding Kansas period. Bushwhackers operated as irregular light cavalry and waged a guerrilla or insurgency war, typically congregating together into bands and living off the land. Unlike regular Confederate cavalry, they often had the finest horses available, which they either stole or bought with loot they had stolen. Missouri bushwhackers Kit Dalton, Cole Younger, and Frank and Jesse James would survive the war to become infamous bank robbers.

FEDERAL

Federal forces in Missouri and Kansas were composed of both US regular army (volunteers) and local militia, including modest numbers of African-Americans, called Colored Volunteers. The bulk of Federal soldiers were from Missouri and Kansas, although Minnesota, Wisconsin, Iowa, Illinois, Indiana, and Colorado all contributed formations. More recent research reveals that small Federal units from as far away as New Jersey, Pennsylvania, and New York also fought at Westport.

By September 1864, most volunteer units of both Missouri and Kansas had been redeployed to the main theaters east of the Mississippi. By the Westport campaign, the combined Federal Departments of Missouri and Kansas were garrisoned by just 14,000 regular troops.

Army of the Department of Missouri

Rosecrans had about 10,000 regular troops stationed throughout the Department of Missouri, although he could call on another 10,000 semi-professional MSM when necessary.

Rosecrans ultimately organized his Department of Missouri field force into a Provisional Cavalry Division of four separate volunteer cavalry brigades. Together these totaled 7,500 cavalry (including 500 mounted Missouri militia) and ten guns.

Army of the Border

Within the Department of Kansas, Curtis had just 4,000 regular troops available at the border. To bolster the department's defenses against invasion, Curtis issued a mandatory call-up of all able-bodied Kansas militia on October 10. About 17,000 militiamen would ultimately muster during the campaign and 15,000 deploy along the border.

Curtis established the Department of Kansas' field force on October 13. This so-called Army of the Border comprised two separate divisions – Major General Blunt's Provisional Cavalry Division and Major General Deitzler's Kansas State Militia Division.

The Kansas Provisional Cavalry Division under Blunt was organized into four brigades, with three brigades comprising Kansas volunteer cavalry and a fourth brigade composed almost entirely of mounted Kansas militia. Blunt's Cavalry Division consisted of about 6,000 cavalry (3,000 volunteer and 3,000 militia) plus 25 artillery guns.

Deitzler's KSM Division comprised 12 unbrigaded Kansas militia regiments, plus three artillery batteries (two Kansas militia and one Colored Volunteer). Altogether Deitzler's KSM Division totaled about 9,000 men and nine guns.

In total, Curtis' Army of the Border comprised about 15,000 men and 34 guns at Westport. Of these, about 3,000 were volunteer cavalry and 12,000 were militia representing 19 KSM regiments.

Federal cavalry

By late 1864, the regular Federal cavalry had matured into a formidable fighting force; its days of being humiliated by its Confederate counterparts were long behind. Federal cavalry weapons were considerably better than their Confederate counterparts. For example, the 11th Kansas Cavalry was armed with 15-shot Henry Rifles rather than single-shot rifles.

Federal cavalry included semi-autonomous scouts, who operated as much as spies as anything else. They both directly tracked Confederate formations and posed as civilians to glean information from locals. Among the Department of Missouri's Federal scouts were 18-year-old Private William F. Cody – the future international showman "Buffalo Bill" – and Cody's 27-year-old civilian friend, James B. "Wild Bill" Hickok.

The Federals often brought superior artillery to battles even when they were outnumbered. Like the Confederates, the Federals were largely a cavalry army and pulled horse artillery and mountain artillery.

Federal infantry

The only significant formation of regular Federal infantry in the campaign was Major General A.J. Smith's XVI Corps, which had been lent to the Department of Missouri but was not formally a part of it.

Missouri militia

Another Samuel J. Reader sketch, this time of the Kansas militia. Most Kansas militiamen were middle-class and working-class civilians, such as farmers, shopkeepers, grocers, lawyers, and doctors. Many had never fired their weapons before they went into combat. (kansasmemory.org, Kansas State Historical Society)

Defending both Missouri and Kansas against bushwhackers and Confederate invasion was largely the responsibility of the various state militias. However, the emergency of Price's invasion would require both states to deploy large numbers of militia against Price's (nominal) professional troops.

Unusually, the state of Missouri had two separate pro-Union militia organizations defending the state.

The Missouri State Militia (MSM) was funded and equipped by the Federal government but only obligated to serve within Missouri. As an anti-guerrilla force, the MSM largely consisted of mounted cavalrymen armed with rifles and pistols; they wore Federal uniforms identical to the volunteer regiments.

The Enrolled Missouri Militia (EMM) was the equivalent of other states' militia or home guard. When portions of the EMM were called up for service, they were known as the Provisional Enrolled Missouri Militia (PEMM). The EMM lacked uniforms and were only identified by a badge.

By late September 1864, Rosecrans had about 24,000 EMM garrisoning towns across Missouri and pursuing pro-Confederate guerrillas. Another 10,000 MSM would eventually consolidate to counter Price's Army of Missouri.

Kansas militia

Kansas had a single militia organization, the Kansas State Militia (KSM). Upon its assembly in mid-October 1864, the KSM was largely issued with new Enfield rifles, and was also well fed and supplied. However, few regulation uniforms were available, meaning most militia would march and fight in their everyday farmer and shopkeeper clothes – in short, they would look exactly like their Confederate enemies. Curtis therefore ordered all Kansas militia not in uniform to distinguish themselves by adding any visibly red material to their coats. Most Kansans responded by plucking and wearing sumac, an ever-present Kansas plant that blazes bright red in the fall. The Kansas militiamen cheerfully called themselves the "Sumac Millish."

ORDERS OF BATTLE

CONFEDERATE

Army of Missouri – Major General Sterling Price (Confederate States Army, CSA)

Fagan's Division – Major General James F. Fagan (CSA)

Cabell's Brigade – Brigadier General William L. Cabell
- Gordon's Arkansas Cavalry – Colonel Anderson Gordon
- Hill's Arkansas Cavalry – Colonel John F. Hill
- Monroe's Arkansas Cavalry – Colonel James C. Monroe
- Morgan's Arkansas Cavalry – Colonel Thomas J. Morgan
- Gunter's Arkansas Cavalry battalion – Lieutenant Colonel Thomas M. Gunter
- Harrell's Arkansas Cavalry battalion – Lieutenant Colonel John M. Harrell
- Witherspoon's Arkansas Cavalry battalion – Major J.L. Witherspoon
- Hughey's Arkansas battery (2x guns) – Captain William M. Hughey

Dobbin's Brigade – Colonel Archibald S. Dobbin
- Dobbin's Arkansas Cavalry – Colonel Archibald S. Dobbin
- McGhee's Arkansas Cavalry – Colonel James H. McGhee (wounded October 23); Lieutenant Colonel Jesse S. Grider
- Witt's Arkansas Cavalry – Colonel A.R. Witt
- Blocher's Arkansas battery (2x guns) – Lieutenant J.V. Zimmerman

Slemons' Brigade – Colonel William F. Slemons
- 2nd Arkansas Cavalry – Colonel William F. Slemons
- Carlton's Arkansas Cavalry – Colonel Charles H. Carlton
- Crawford's Arkansas Cavalry – Colonel William A. Crawford
- Wright's Arkansas Cavalry – Colonel John C. Wright

McCray's Brigade – Colonel Thomas H. McCray
- 15th Missouri Cavalry – Colonel Timothy Reves
- 45th Arkansas Infantry (mounted) – Colonel Milton D. Baber
- 47th Arkansas Infantry (mounted) – Colonel Lee Crandall

Lyle's Arkansas Cavalry – Colonel Oliver P. Lyle
- Rogan's Arkansas Cavalry – Colonel James W. Rogan
- Anderson's Arkansas Cavalry battalion – Captain William L. Anderson

Marmaduke's Division – Major General John S. Marmaduke (CSA)

Marmaduke's escort: Company D, 5th Missouri Cavalry – Captain D.R. Stallard

Marmaduke's Brigade – Brigadier General John B. Clark, Jr.
- 3rd Missouri Cavalry – Colonel Colton Greene
- 4th Missouri Cavalry – Colonel John Q. Burbridge
- 7th Missouri Cavalry – Colonel Solomon G. Kitchen
- 8th Missouri Cavalry – Colonel William L. Jeffers
- 10th Missouri Cavalry – Colonel Robert R. Lawther
- 14th Missouri Cavalry battalion – Lieutenant Colonel J.F. Davies
- Hogan's Engineer company – Captain James T. Hogan

Freeman's Brigade – Colonel Thomas R. Freeman
- Freeman's Missouri Cavalry – Lieutenant Colonel Joseph R. Love
- Fristoe's Missouri Cavalry – Colonel Edward T. Fristoe
- Ford's Arkansas Cavalry battalion – Lieutenant Colonel Barney Ford

Harris' Missouri battery (1x gun) – Lieutenant T.J. Williams

Hynson's Texas battery (4x guns) – Captain Henry C. Hynson

Shelby's Division – Brigadier General Joseph O. Shelby (CSA)

Shelby's Iron Brigade – Brigadier General M. Jeff Thompson
- 5th Missouri Cavalry – Colonel Frank B. Gordon
- 11th Missouri Cavalry – Colonel Moses W. Smith
- 12th Missouri Cavalry – Lieutenant Colonel William H. Erwin
- Elliot's Missouri Cavalry – Colonel Benjamin F. Elliot
- Crisp's Cavalry battalion – Lieutenant Colonel John T. Crisp
- Johnson's Cavalry battalion – Major Rector Johnson
- Slayback's Missouri Cavalry battalion – Lieutenant Colonel Alonzo Slayback
- Collins' Missouri battery (2x guns) – Captain Richard A. Collins

Jackman's Brigade – Colonel Sidney D. Jackman
- Hunter's Missouri Cavalry – Colonel DeWitt C. Hunter
- Jackman's Missouri Cavalry – Lieutenant Colonel C.H. Nichols
- Schnable's Missouri Cavalry battalion – Lieutenant Colonel John A. Schnable
- Williams' Missouri Cavalry battalion – Lieutenant Colonel D.A. Williams
- Collins' Missouri battery (detachment) (2x guns) – Lieutenant Jacob D. Connor

Tyler's Brigade – Colonel Charles H. Tyler
- Coffee's Missouri Cavalry – Colonel J.T. Coffee
- Perkins' Missouri Cavalry – Colonel Caleb Perkins
- Searcey's Missouri Cavalry – Colonel James T. Searcey
- Unorganized recruits

46th Arkansas Infantry (mounted) – Colonel W.O. Coleman

FEDERAL

Department of Kansas: Army of the Border – Major General Samuel R. Curtis (USA)

Curtis' escort: Company G, 11th Kansas Cavalry and battery (2x guns) – Lieutenant Edward Gill

Major Robert H. Hunt, Chief of Artillery

Provisional Cavalry Division – Major General James G. Blunt (USA)

1st Brigade – Colonel Charles R. "Doc" Jennison (15th Kansas Cavalry)
- 15th Kansas Cavalry – Captain Robert Carpenter
- 3rd Wisconsin Cavalry (detachment) – Captain Robert Carpenter
- Foster's Missouri Cavalry battalion – Captain George S. Grover
- Battery (5x guns), manned by 15th Kansas Cavalry – Lieutenant Henry L. Barker

2nd Brigade – Colonel Thomas Moonlight (11th Kansas Cavalry)
- 11th Kansas Cavalry – Lieutenant Colonel Preston B. Plumb
- 5th Kansas Cavalry (Companies L and M) – Captain James H. Young
- 16th Kansas Cavalry (Companies A and D) – Lieutenant Colonel Samuel Walker
- Battery (4x guns), manned by Company E, 11th Kansas Cavalry

3rd Brigade – Colonel Charles W. Blair (14th Kansas Cavalry)
- 4th Kansas Militia – Colonel W.D. McCain
- 5th Kansas Militia – Colonel G.A. Colton
- 6th Kansas Militia – Colonel James D. Snoddy (arrested October 16); Colonel James H. Montgomery
- 10th Kansas Militia – Colonel William Pennock
- 19th Kansas Militia – Colonel A.C. Hogan
- 24th Kansas Militia (battalion) – Lieutenant Colonel George Eaves
- 14th Kansas Cavalry (Company E) – Lieutenant William B. Clark
- 9th Wisconsin Battery (6x guns) – Captain James H. Dodge
- 2nd Kansas State Artillery (2x guns) – Lieutenant Daniel C. Knowles

4th Brigade – Colonel James H. Ford (2nd Colorado Cavalry)
- 2nd Colorado Cavalry – Major J. Nelson Smith (killed October 21); Major J.H. Pritchard
- 16th Kansas Cavalry (detachment) – Major James Ketner
- McLain's Independent Colorado Battery (6x guns) – Captain W.D. McLain

KSM Division – Major General George W. Deitzler (Adjutant General of Kansas)

Brigadier General M.S. Grant (Kansas Militia)

Brigadier General William H.M. Fishback (Kansas Militia)
- 1st Kansas Militia – Colonel Charles H. Robinson
- 2nd Kansas Militia – Colonel George W. Veale

2nd Kansas Colored Militia – Captain James L. Rafferty, Captain Richard L. Hinton
- 7th Kansas Militia – Colonel Peter McFarland
- 9th Kansas Militia – Colonel Frank M. Tracy
- 12th Kansas Militia – Colonel L.S. Treat
- 13th Kansas Militia – Colonel Alexander S. Johnson

14th Kansas Militia – Colonel William Gordon
18th Kansas Militia – Colonel Matthew Quigg
20th Kansas Militia – Colonel J.B. Hubbell
21st Kansas Militia – Colonel Sandy Lowe
22nd Kansas Militia – Colonel William Weer
Independent Colored Battery (6x guns) – Captain H. Ford Douglas
Zesch's Battery, Kansas Militia Light Artillery (2x guns) – Captain Gustavus Zesch
Topeka Battery, 2nd Kansas Militia (1x gun) – Captain Ross Burnes
Kansas City Home Guards – Colonel Kersey Coates

Army of the Department of Missouri – Major General William S. Rosecrans (USA)

Provisional Cavalry Division – Major General Alfred S. Pleasonton (USA)
Colonel Nelson Cole (2nd Missouri Light Artillery), Chief of Artillery
1st Brigade – Brigadier General Egbert B. Brown (arrested October 23); Colonel John F. Philips (7th Missouri Militia Cavalry)
1st Missouri Militia Cavalry – Colonel James McFerran (arrested October 23); Lieutenant Colonel Bazel Lazear
4th Missouri Militia Cavalry – Major George W. Kelly
7th Missouri Militia Cavalry – Colonel John F. Philips, Lieutenant Colonel Thomas T. Crittenden
1st Iowa Cavalry (detachment) – Major John McDermott
2nd Brigade – Brigadier General John McNeil
5th Missouri Militia Cavalry – Lieutenant Colonel Joseph Eppstein
7th Kansas Cavalry – Major Francis Malone
13th Missouri Cavalry – Colonel Edwin C. Catherwood
17th Illinois Cavalry – Colonel John L. Beveridge
2nd Missouri Cavalry (detachment) – Captain George M. Houston
3rd Missouri Militia Cavalry (detachment) – Lieutenant Colonel Henry M. Matthews
9th Missouri Militia Cavalry (detachment) – Lieutenant Colonel Daniel M. Draper
3rd Brigade – Brigadier General John B. Sanborn
2nd Arkansas Cavalry – Colonel John E. Phelps
8th Missouri Militia Cavalry – Colonel Joseph J. Gravely
6th Missouri Militia Cavalry (detachment) – Major William Plumb
6th EMM Cavalry (detachment) – Lieutenant Colonel John F. McMahan
7th EMM Cavalry (detachment) – Major W.B. Mitchell
4th Brigade – Colonel Edward F. Winslow (4th Iowa Cavalry) (wounded October 23); Lieutenant Colonel Frederick W. Benteen (10th Missouri Cavalry)
3rd Iowa Cavalry – Major Benjamin S. Jones
4th Iowa Cavalry – Major Abial R. Pierce
10th Missouri Cavalry – Lieutenant Colonel Frederick W. Benteen, Major William H. Lusk
4th Missouri Cavalry (detachment) – Captain George D. Knispel
7th Indiana Cavalry (detachment) – Major S.W. Simonsen
Company H, 2nd Missouri Light Artillery (2x guns) – Captain William C.F. Montgomery, Lieutenant Philip Smiley
Company L, 2nd Missouri Light Artillery (4x guns) – Captain Charles H. Thurber
Battery, 5th Missouri Militia Cavalry (2x guns) – Lieutenant Adam Hillerich
2nd New Jersey Cavalry (detachment) – Captain Michael Gallagher
19th Pennsylvania Cavalry (one company)

XVI Corps – Major General A.J. Smith (USA)
1st Division (detachment) – Colonel Joseph J. Woods
2nd Brigade – Colonel Lucius F. Hubbard (5th Minnesota Infantry)
5th Minnesota Infantry
7th Minnesota Infantry
8th Wisconsin Infantry
9th Minnesota Infantry
10th Minnesota Infantry
12th Iowa Infantry
47th Illinois Infantry
Battery G, 2nd Illinois Light Artillery
3rd Division (detachment) – Colonel David Moore
1st Brigade – Colonel T.J. Kinney (119th Illinois Infantry)
58th Illinois Infantry
89th Indiana Infantry
119th Illinois Infantry
2nd Brigade – Colonel James I. Gilbert (27th Iowa Infantry)
14th Iowa Infantry
24th Missouri Infantry
27th Iowa Infantry
32nd Iowa Infantry
3rd Brigade – Colonel Edward H. Wolfe (52nd Indiana Infantry)
49th Illinois Infantry
52nd Indiana Infantry
117th Illinois Infantry
178th New York Infantry
3rd Indiana Battery
9th Indiana Battery

OPPOSING PLANS

WEATHER AND TERRAIN

By late September 1864, the usual hot, humid, and meteorologically violent Kansas and Missouri summer would give way to a cool and clear fall, the region's only truly pleasant season for overland marching. However, by late October, the climax of the campaign, the weather would grow legitimately cold, with the Federal XVI Corps marching through snow in central Missouri, and the Kansas City area's streams and creeks noticeably crusted over with ice during the Westport battle. Snow flurries accompanied the troops at times, while a violent prairie thunderstorm would batter the armies the night before the decisive October 25 cavalry battles.

Encompassing southern Missouri are the mountainous and heavily wooded Ozarks, an ancient volcanic plateau climbing from the south bank of the Missouri River to the 1,772ft St. Francois Mountains of southeastern Missouri. The Ozarks ultimately extend into northern Arkansas, where the more rugged Boston Mountains rise to 2,560ft and are cut by valleys up to 1,500ft deep. An agriculturally and economically impoverished region, the Ozarks were unsuitable for plantation agriculture and therefore far removed

A 2006 view of the Missouri Ozarks' St. Francois Mountains, 15 miles to the northeast of Pilot Knob, illustrates the difficult southeast Missouri terrain Price's army marched through en route to St. Louis. (Kbh3rd, CC BY-3.0 https://creativecommons.org/licenses/by-sa/3.0, via Wikimedia Commons)

from slave-ownership – paradoxically making sparsely populated southern Missouri strongly Unionist.

Additionally, this virtually undeveloped mountain wilderness was a major obstacle. Price's Army of Missouri would skirt the Ozarks' southeastern edge en route to St. Louis. The Ozarks and the even more rugged 2,753ft Ouachita Mountains, farther south in western Arkansas and eastern Indian Territory (modern-day Oklahoma), would also prove an obstacle upon Price's eventual retirement south at the end of the campaign.

In contrast, the stereotypically Midwestern landscape of western Missouri and adjoining eastern Kansas comprises gently rolling hills, rich farmland, vast stretches of tallgrass prairie, and patches of oak-hickory timberlands sliced by meandering creeks and rivers.

The future Kansas City, Missouri, was founded in the 1830s on the western Missouri border where the Kansas River flows into the Missouri River. By 1860, Kansas City's population had grown to 4,418. Three miles south of Kansas City on the Missouri side of the border was the village of Westport, founded in 1833 and with an 1860 population of 1,195. Like Kansas City, Westport functioned as a frontier staging post for westward expansion.

CONFEDERATE

Although the Army of Missouri's 1864 expedition has become known as "Price's Raid," the campaign as intended and executed was a Confederate invasion of Missouri; its primary objective, however remote, was the capture of St. Louis and the holding of elections for the Confederate Missouri government-in-exile.

On August 4, 1864, Major General Edmund Kirby Smith cut his orders to Price:

> Rally the loyal men of Missouri, and remember that our great want is men ... Make St. Louis the objective point of your movement, which, if rapidly made, will put you in possession of that place, its supplies, and military stores, and which will do more toward rallying Missouri to your standard than the possession of any other point. Should you be compelled to withdraw from the State, make your retreat through Kansas and the Indian Territory, sweeping that country of its mules, horses, cattle, and military supplies of all kinds.

Considering Missouri friendly territory, Smith further ordered Price to "avoid all wanton acts of destruction and devastation, restrain your men, and impress upon them that their aim should be to secure success in a just and holy cause and not to gratify personal feeling and revenge."

In the likely event that a Missouri occupation would be fleeting, Price planned his outbound ravaging of Kansas to include the sacking of the state's Fort Leavenworth and Fort Scott.

FEDERAL

Federal grand strategy required a continuation of a purely defensive policy in the Trans-Mississippi Theater. Indeed, in June 1864, Grant wrote to

Halleck: "West of the Mississippi I would not attempt anything until the rebellion east of it is entirely subdued." Grant recognized the war would be decided by destroying Lee's Army of Northern Virginia and Johnston's Army of Tennessee. He therefore decided to concentrate all possible Federal strength in the East at the expense of Federal forces west of the Mississippi. Lincoln concurred with Grant's strategy, noting, "If a man can't skin, he must hold a leg while someone else does."

Indeed by 1864, many Federal officials believed the coordinated Confederate war effort in Missouri and Kansas might be over. The Federal Departments of Missouri and Kansas were therefore unprepared for a major Confederate operation into their states.

Rosecrans had less than 10,000 troops to defend Missouri and these were dispersed throughout the state. While intelligence eventually made Rosecrans aware of Price's upcoming operation, Rosecrans was unsure of Price's location or intentions. As late as September 22, Rosecrans would inform Curtis, "Our information does not yet warrant much southward movement to meet Price, whose line of movement is not yet developed."

The Department of Kansas was equally unprepared for a significant Confederate invasion. Nearly 20 percent of Kansas' land area comprised Indian reservations. In July 1864, the Kansas plains had erupted into the Cheyenne War, forcing Curtis to mostly concentrate on defending his vast department against Plains Indian raids, rather than the increasingly scarce bushwhacker raids, or the least likely scenario of all, an organized Confederate invasion of Kansas.

The modern-day Kansas State Capitol in Topeka, 2024. Federal plans to defend against Price were handicapped by Kansas' dysfunctional political situation. The state's moderate Republican governor in 1864, Thomas Carney, feared reports of a Confederate invasion were a cynical ploy by Jim Lane's Radical Republicans to interfere with the scheduled November elections. (Nils Huenerfuerst, CC BY SA 4.0 https://creativecommons.org/licenses/by/4.0, via Wikimedia Commons)

THE CAMPAIGN

PRICE'S ARMY OF MISSOURI DEPARTS, AUGUST 28–SEPTEMBER 19

In late August 1864, General Kirby Smith ordered his Confederate infantry to feint against Little Rock while Shelby's cavalry raided Federal communications in northeastern Arkansas. These actions sufficiently distracted Federal attention, allowing Price's army to slip past the Federal defensive line. On August 29, Price successfully rendezvoused with Marmaduke's and Fagan's Divisions at Princeton, Arkansas.

The start of the campaign had already been delayed by tardy reception of supplies from Shreveport. Now Price led the Army of Missouri northeast with a seeming lack of urgency. Price himself rarely rode in the saddle, often traveling by carriage instead. Progress was further slowed by Price making "eloquent speeches along the way." The languid pace allowed reports of Price's march to make their way to Federal authorities.

At this time, Major General A.J. Smith's Federal XVI Corps was being shipped up the Mississippi from Memphis to the Tennessee River, to eventually reinforce Sherman's drive on Atlanta. On September 3, Rosecrans requested a detachment from XVI Corps, resulting in a Federal division being moved upriver towards Cape Girardeau to help reinforce St. Louis.

Meanwhile, Price's men crossed the Arkansas River at Dardanelle on September 7. A frustrated Major General Steele, commanding Federal forces in Arkansas, duly reported that Price had crossed the Arkansas with a large cavalry force of between 5,000 and 10,000 men, and correctly deduced that Price intended to rendezvous with Shelby, who Steele reported as having 5,000 armed cavalrymen. However, despite reports of Price's men claiming their objective was Missouri, Steele found it difficult to believe how the army could subsist on a march to Missouri. Having belatedly received reinforcements from Memphis, Steele nevertheless promised to "do all I can to keep Price out of Missouri" while complaining he lacked sufficient cavalry to handle Price's army, and that his infantry would be unlikely to catch it.

The Marmaduke and Fagan Divisions, accompanied by Price, arrived at Pocahontas, Arkansas, on September 14, where they were joined by Shelby's Division on September 17. Price's men had traveled 324 miles in 18 days. They had averaged just 18 miles a day, an ominously slow pace for cavalry.

Price now re-organized the Army of Missouri into three divisions under Fagan, Marmaduke, and Shelby. Shelby's Division would march on the left,

Fagan's Division in the center, and Marmaduke's on the right, with Shelby and Marmaduke ranging 10–20 miles from Fagan's center.

The following day, September 18, saw Price's troops skirmish with Lieutenant Erich Pape's 80 men of the 3rd Missouri State Cavalry, establishing that a major Confederate invasion was headed towards Missouri. The next day, September 19, Price's army crossed into Missouri.

PRICE INVADES MISSOURI, SEPTEMBER 20–OCTOBER 7

Major General Rosecrans' Department of Missouri had just shy of 10,000 Federal troops available throughout the state. Of the department's five districts, the most important for the initial defense against Price was the District of St. Louis, encompassing the eastern stretch of Missouri along the banks of the Mississippi River. The St. Louis district totaled about 3,200 troops, divided into three sub-districts. Defending the city of St. Louis itself was Sub-District I, totaling over 1,500 troops. Cape Girardeau and New Madrid – Mississippi River towns in the state's far southeast – were defended by the combined 650 troops of Sub-District II. Finally, garrisoning the Pilot Knob area were just over 1,000 troops of Sub-District III.

On September 20, the Shelby Division encountered about 75 Federal cavalry at Doniphan, Missouri, and were then briefly harassed by Federal militia at Patterson, Missouri, on September 22. Shelby's men easily drove off both enemy parties, but the initial September 20 contact was promptly reported to the Federal outpost at Pilot Knob's Fort Davidson.

Major James Wilson commanded Sub-District III from Fort Davidson, then garrisoned by just 150 Federal troops. On September 23, Wilson messaged Brigadier General Ewing: "Citizens report Shelby, with 8,000 men, on the Whitewater, twenty miles from Fredericktown, yesterday. I cannot believe the report to be true."

Nevertheless, by September 24, Rosecrans finally accepted there was a Confederate threat to St. Louis. Rosecrans ordered Brigadier General Ewing to concentrate at Pilot Knob and Cape Girardeau. By September 25, Major Wilson would consolidate the full 1,000 troops under his command. Meanwhile, Ewing moved south towards Pilot Knob with part of a regiment.

Price's three columns successfully rendezvoused at Fredericktown over September 24–25. Price was now just 90 miles south of his objective, St. Louis. However, his confidence in attacking St. Louis was shaken when he received a false report that A.J. Smith's XVI Corps was encamped ten miles outside St. Louis with about 8,000 Federal infantry.

A second disconcerting report followed from Shelby's scouts: nearby Fort Davidson was garrisoned by about 1,500 Federal troops. Shelby urged bypassing the fort and heading for St. Louis, but Fagan convinced Price to capture the fort rather than leave it intact to his rear. Price's exact motives are unknown, but he may have believed capturing Fort Davidson would be an easy victory to boost his men's morale.

The battle of Fort Davidson, September 27–28

Fort Davidson was a hexagonal fortress mounting four 32-pounder siege guns and three 24-pounder howitzers, and lying just outside the southeast

Missouri town of Pilot Knob. However, Fort Davidson was unhappily situated in rugged Ozark terrain and totally encircled by hills, making it highly vulnerable to bombardment from well-placed artillery.

Commanding Fort Davidson was Brigadier General Thomas Ewing, Jr., whose total garrison came to 1,051 Federal troops and 150 armed civilians. However, the only combat-tested veterans were five companies of the 14th Iowa Infantry, totaling just 562 men.

Although badly outnumbered, Ewing vowed to stubbornly hold Fort Davidson as long as possible to delay Price's general advance into Missouri. Ewing knew his men's likely reward – those who survived – was to be captured.

Price ordered the Fagan and Marmaduke Divisions to make the main assault against Fort Davidson. Shelby's mission would be to cut off potential Federal reinforcements to the beleaguered fort. Shelby would thus flank wide to the north of Pilot Knob to cut the Iron Mountain Railroad, Ewing's line of communication to St. Louis.

Brigadier General Thomas Ewing, Jr. was 35 years old during Price's expedition and already well hated by the Confederates for carrying out General Order No. 11, which resulted in the "Burnt District" of four Missouri counties on the Kansas border. Transferred to southeast Missouri, Ewing would show steely resolve defending Fort Davidson at the outset of the Westport campaign. (Civil War photographs, 1861–1865, Library of Congress, Prints and Photographs Division)

Early on September 26, Price sent the Fagan and Marmaduke Divisions towards Ironton and Pilot Knob. Price simultaneously sent a Fagan detachment to seize a difficult pass between two mountains three miles from Ironton. By evening of the September 26, Fagan's men had driven the Federal pickets near Arcadia into the town. The following day, September 27, Fagan's and Marmaduke's troops decisively threw back Major Wilson's forward detachment and secured the gap between Pilot Knob and Shepherd's Mountain.

Price now offered Ewing a chance to surrender. Ewing refused, possibly fearing he would be executed for his issuing of the notorious General Order No. 11 the previous year. Confederate cannon opened up, and Price's main attack against Fort Davidson finally began at 1400hrs on the afternoon of September 27. Perhaps 4,700 Confederate troops were directly

Fort Davidson seen in a modern-day view in April 2010. The high Ozark hills surrounding the fort are apparent; it was from here that Price's men descended into the plain surrounding the fort to attack it. On October 3, 1864, Price's Confederates would execute Major James Wilson and five other Federals captured at Fort Davidson. (Kbh3rd, CC BY 3.0 https://creativecommons.org/licenses/by/3.0, via Wikimedia Commons)

Battle of Fort Davidson, September 27–28

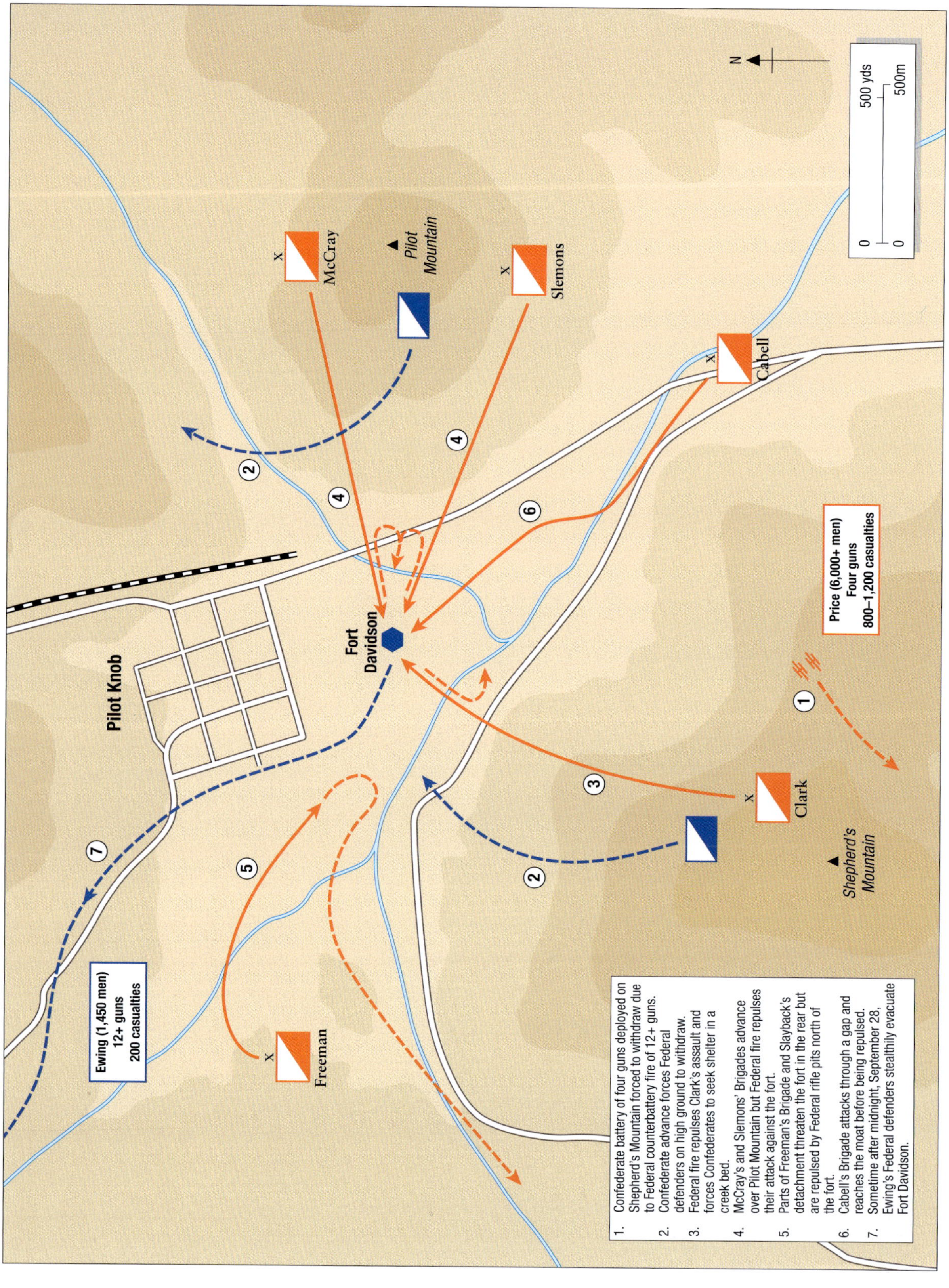

available for the assault. The Fagan and Marmaduke Divisions were to attack simultaneously from multiple sides. However, Marmaduke's troops were advancing downhill from the rocky terrain of Shepherd's Mountain, ensuring that Fagan's troops reached the fort first. Fagan's men now found themselves exposed and alone on the flat 300-acre plain in front of the fort, and were quickly subjected to withering fire. Most of the Fagan Division fled in retreat. The only exception was the Cabell Brigade, which made it to the ditch surrounding the fort before also being repulsed. Meanwhile, most of the Marmaduke Division had taken cover in a dry creek bed below Shepherd's Mountain and barely participated in the assault.

Ewing had repelled the first Confederate assault, but had suffered 200 casualties. Ewing had additionally received a Confederate message announcing that Ewing's Colored Volunteers would be summarily executed upon capture. Unable to resist a second major attack, Ewing resolved to somehow evacuate his men.

Just after midnight, in the early dark of September 28, the Fort Davidson drawbridge was lowered and Ewing's Federal garrison began creeping across, their footfalls and wagon wheels muffled by laid-down tents and the ongoing misty rain. Price's men were none the wiser and two hours later Ewing's escaping rearguard detonated Fort Davidson's magazine. By then, Ewing's men had slipped through Price's cordon and were en route to Caledonia.

Believing the magazine detonation an accident, Price waited several hours for presumably dazed Federal survivors to surrender. Only at 0800hrs did Price realize the fort had been abandoned. A pursuit was not organized until 1000hrs, too late to be of any use. Confederate casualties approached a staggering 1,000 killed or wounded. Price had taken Fort Davidson, but it had been a pyrrhic victory the expedition could ill afford.

Price's Army of Missouri approaches St. Louis, September 28–October 1

On October 1, the Army of Missouri briefly occupied Franklin, just 40 miles west of downtown St. Louis. That same day Price's men captured the town of Washington on the southern bank of the Missouri River. However, the Missouri itself was too great an obstacle, ending Price's advance north.

Price now had to make a decision. St. Louis held the promise of huge quantities of military provisions. Additionally, capturing the eighth-largest city in the country, even for a brief period, would be a huge political blow to Union morale during the critical election period, and a magnificent feather in Price's cap.

However, Price believed St. Louis to be heavily garrisoned, a natural assumption based on its strategic importance. In fact, like Missouri at large, St. Louis was weakly defended, a product of Grant's and Lincoln's strategy to scour all possible Federal strength from the war's peripheries to mass at the decisive theaters in the East. The result was that a single division of A.J. Smith's XVI Corps was set up along the Meramec River, with barely 1,500 additional troops inside the city of St. Louis itself. Of these, most were EMM. Because St. Louis had not been significantly menaced since 1862, the local militia had lapsed into a state of poor training and organization. None had ever seen combat.

However, perhaps shaken by his costly frontal assault on Fort Davidson, Price suddenly abandoned the longstanding plan to capture St. Louis. While it

James "Wild Bill" Hickok seen near the time of the Price expedition. Hickok had volunteered for US Army service in 1861 and by July 1864 was operating as a civilian scout for Brigadier General John McNeil. Hickok's good friend "Buffalo Bill" Cody, also operating as a Federal scout, claimed to have run into Hickok by chance, probably near the Gasconade River around October 4–5, 1864. According to Cody, Hickok was disguised as a Confederate officer with the Marmaduke Division. The two chatted for a while before Hickok briefed Cody on Price's operations. Hickok insisted on spying on Price for a while longer, but handed Cody a package of letters for Cody to deliver to McNeil. Cody agreed, and the two friends shook hands and departed. (Bettmann/Contributor, via Getty Images)

is impossible to know the outcome of an attack that never happened, Price's decision may have been one of the Confederacy's great lost opportunities. If Price had taken St. Louis, it would have been by far the largest Union city captured by the Confederacy throughout the war; indeed St. Louis was 12 times larger than Harrisburg, Pennsylvania, which General Lee's Army of Northern Virginia had occupied in June 1863. The consistently hapless Price may have suddenly become one of the most lionized Confederate heroes of the war.

Advance to Jefferson City, October 1–8

Price's alternative, Jefferson City, was a modest town of 4,000 and nowhere as militarily rich a target as St. Louis. However, it was presumably much less well defended. Indeed, occupying an important Missouri city and holding elections had been one of Price's assigned objectives for the campaign. Additionally, capturing Jefferson City, the Missouri state capital, would be a major political coup.

Despite later claiming that he "was determined to move as fast as possible on Jefferson City," Price set off towards the Missouri capital at his usual leisurely pace. Because the Army of Missouri lacked any communication lines, it was forced to forage the countryside to stay alive. By pillaging the towns along its route, the Army of Missouri ensured that its secondary objective, that of winning over the local Missouri population, was essentially lost from the outset.

By October 3, Federal scouts – including the future James "Wild Bill" Hickok – were reporting Price's destination as Jefferson City, prompting the Federals to concentrate nearby local militias there. Defenseless, most Missouri communities in Price's path were compelled to surrender without a shot fired. However, Hermann, a German-American town of 1,100 in the Missouri Rhineland region, offered a rare resistance to Price's forces before it was taken by Marmaduke on October 3. Hermann's fervently Unionist German immigrants were widely hated by Missouri Confederates. Some of Price's men, likely acting independently, would execute several civilians for being prominent Unionists or for simply being German.

Price's offensive across Missouri now resembled a race, with Price's Army of Missouri driving west across the state, and Rosecrans' scattered Federal outposts across eastern Missouri attempting to marshal in pursuit. However, Price's army, already disappointingly slow marchers by mounted standards, continued to accumulate more and more plunder, slowing them even further. Indeed, Price's original train of 300 wagons had by now bloated to 500 wagons and 5,000 cattle.

Back on October 1, Jefferson City had lacked any entrenchments and had been defended by a garrison of only 1,000 men, of whom half were poorly equipped and untrained EMM. However, under Brigadier Generals John Brown and Clinton Fisk, the Jefferson City garrison began to dig defensive entrenchments and by October 4 Jefferson City's defenders had increased from 1,000 to 5,000 troops, although half were EMM.

Rosecrans had ordered Brigadier General John McNeil to stay put and defend Rolla – Rosecrans' last communication to McNeil before Price's Confederates cut the telegraph line. However, late on October 3, McNeil divined Price's intentions to advance on Jefferson City. Without orders, McNeil decided on his own accord to move his and Brigadier General John

Sanborn's men to Jefferson City, marching out of Rolla early on October 4. This resulted in a combined 3,000 well-trained troops and six guns en route to reinforce the threatened capital.

The wily 18-year-old William F. Cody, a scout in the 7th Kansas Cavalry who in later years would become world famous as "Buffalo Bill." Cody had been assigned to report to Brigadier General John Sanborn. Both "Buffalo Bill" and "Wild Bill" were involved as Federal scouts/spies during the Westport campaign, although their exact contributions remain obscure, as one would expect from their job. (Photo by Gado/Getty Images)

Price's Army of Missouri was now approaching. On October 5, Marmaduke's forward detachments reached and burned the Pacific Railroad bridge on the Gasconade River; the bridge had been abandoned by the 34th EMM the previous night. Simultaneously, Confederate troops also skirmished with EMM units at the Osage River Railroad bridge.

By now Jefferson City had been reinforced to 7,000 pro-Union defenders. The following day, October 6, McNeil's and Sanborn's Federal Brigades arrived at Jefferson City. That same day, Brigadier General Fisk received telegraphed orders to assume command of the full Jefferson City garrison. Fisk organized his available forces into four brigades. Three were commanded by Brigadier Generals Egbert Brown, John McNeil, and John Sanborn, while the fourth was assigned to Colonel Franklin W. Hickox of the EMM.

McNeil's and Sanborn's Brigades immediately marched east to defend the Osage River, which flowed north into the Missouri River seven miles downstream of Jefferson City. McNeil deployed his men across an eight-mile stretch to defend multiple crossing sites. They were promptly attacked by Shelby's Division, which pinned the Federals at Prince's Ford and Bolton's Ford while concentrating the main assault at Castle Rock Ford. Overwhelmed, McNeil's and Sanborn's Federals fell back stubbornly. During the running battle they managed to kill Colonel David Shanks, commander of Shelby's famed Iron Brigade. By nightfall, October 6, Shelby's men had successfully crossed the Osage River in the face of outnumbered Union resistance and pushed the Federal defenders back into Jefferson City. Shelby's men were camped just a few miles outside Jefferson City.

As October 7 dawned, the situation looked grim for the Federal defenders. Throughout the previous day's fighting they had hoped to be rescued by elements of Major General A.J. Smith's XVI Corps. However, Rosecrans had so far only concentrated one of the XVI Corps' two divisions at Kirkwood, just west of St. Louis. The remaining division, under Brigadier General Mower, was still as far south as Cape Girardeau and marching as fast as it could under trying conditions. Smith was wary of heading west until his force was properly concentrated, meaning Jefferson City's gallant defenders would have to repel the Confederate invaders on their own. By now, the total Federal garrison at Jefferson City came to 7,200 men in four brigades. As senior officer present, Fisk was placed in command of the whole garrison.

Price's Army of Missouri contingent facing Jefferson City numbered about 12,000 men, almost twice that of the Federal defenders. However, pro-Confederate spies inside Jefferson City had badly overestimated the size of the defending Federal force; they reported to Price a total Jefferson City garrison of 12,000 defenders, equal to Price's own, with another 3,000 having supposedly just arrived on the opposite bank of the Missouri River. Additionally, under Brigadier General Egbert Brown, the Federals had developed heavy entrenchments in just a matter of days, having "repaired the two partially constructed forts ... [and] built three substantial new ones"

Major General A.J. Smith, commander of the US Army's XVI Corps. Smith's XVI Corps detachment was the only major formation of regular infantry to participate in the Westport campaign, although orders from superiors made it difficult for his men to get engaged in the action. (piemags/CMB, via Alamy Stock Photo)

as well as building "nearly three miles of entrenchments, palisades, rifle-pits, [and] cheveaux-de-frise [obstacles]."

On the morning of October 7, Price's Army of Missouri commanded the heights above Jefferson City. As the Confederates and Federals exchanged desultory fire, Price and his officers observed the situation. They saw heavy fortifications protecting the city and imagined it was manned by a force equal or superior in numbers to themselves. After Pilot Knob, Price was reluctant to order another direct assault into heavy defenses. After a council of war with his divisional commanders, Price ordered the Army of Missouri to withdraw and march towards Boonville.

With Price's decision to bypass Jefferson City, the primary mission of the Missouri invasion had irredeemably failed. Neither St. Louis nor Jefferson City had been captured. There would be no installation and elections of a pro-Confederate government. Missouri remained firmly part of the Union. The only remaining course of action available to Price was to invade Kansas and cause as much damage as possible during the withdrawal south.

MISSOURI BUSHWHACKER ACTIONS, JULY 23–OCTOBER 9

Confederate bushwhackers had been highly active in central Missouri throughout the summer. Although many bands were involved, the most prominent was that of the original Quantrill's Raiders, now commanded by Bloody Bill Anderson. Among Anderson's band were future outlaw brothers Frank and Jesse James, who had recently joined Anderson that summer.

On July 23, Anderson's guerrillas raided the villages of Renick and Allen, then defeated a pursuing cavalry detachment. Anderson then razed the towns of Shelbina and Lakenan on July 27 and burned the Salt River Railroad bridge.

Then on August 28, Anderson lured and ambushed a band of 54 Federal troops near Rocheport, Boone County, with about a hundred of his own bushwhackers. Seven Federals were killed, all left scalped or with their throats cut. Over the subsequent two weeks Anderson's guerrillas would operate out of the Rocheport area and attack steamboats on the Missouri River. Finally on September 8, Anderson received official orders from the Confederate government to support the Price invasion by harassing Federal lines of communication.

On September 23, Anderson's men raided Rocheport itself, killing 11 Federal soldiers and three black civilian teamsters. Local militia then executed six of Anderson's men captured near Rocheport.

The following day, September 24, three different bushwhacker chieftains – Bloody Bill Anderson, George Todd, and Dave Poole – combined their bands into a force of about 400 men and attacked the town of Fayette. Quantrill had been invited but refused, claiming Fayette too heavily defended. Quantrill proved correct – the Fayette attack failed badly, leading to the bushwhackers losing 13 dead and 30 wounded to just one Federal killed. Defeated, the combined bushwhacker group dispersed.

Bloody Bill Anderson's guerrilla raids, July 23–October 9

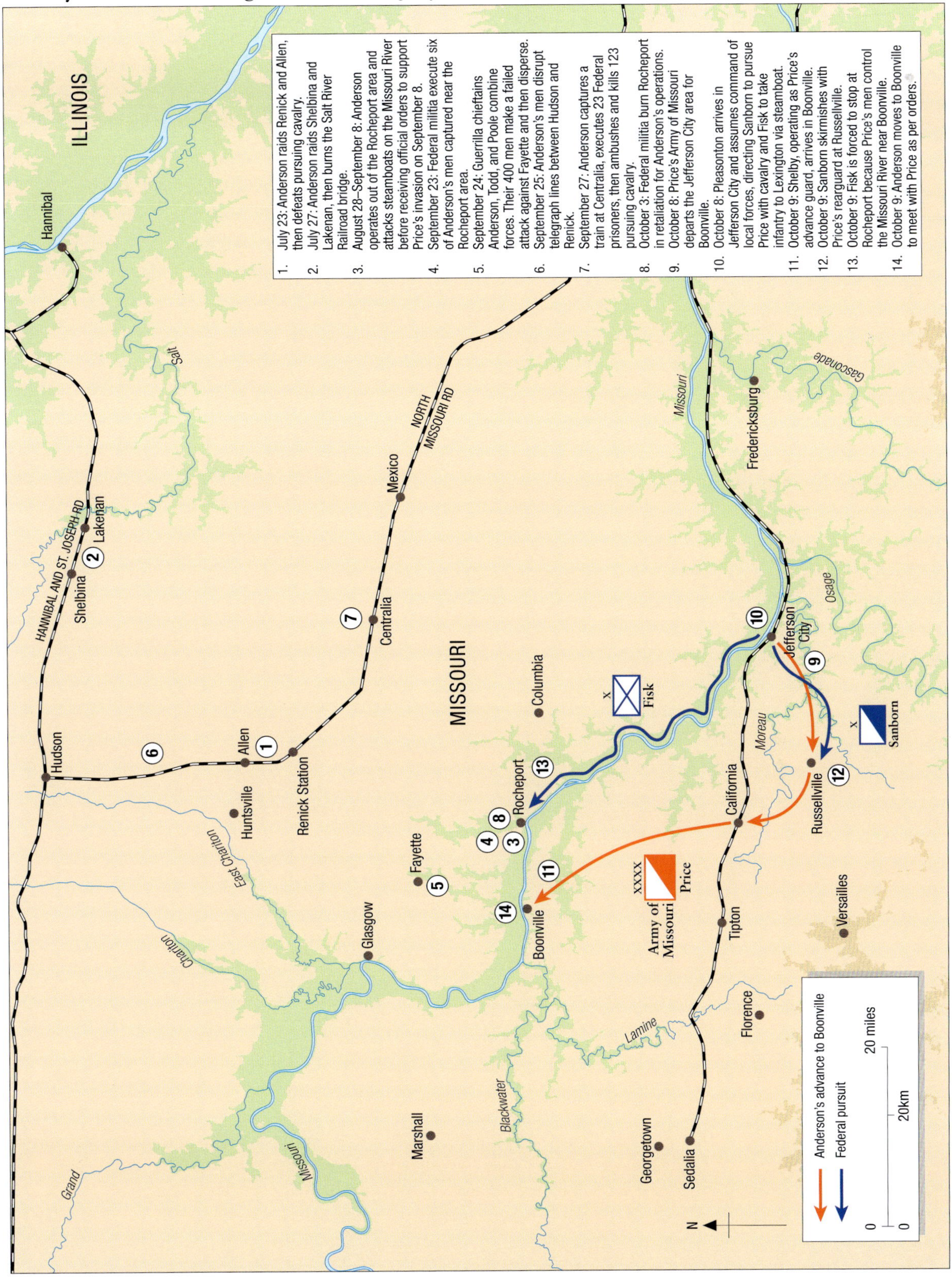

LEFT
A former Kansan born into a Southern family, the 24-year-old William "Bloody Bill" Anderson was arguably the most brutal Missouri bushwhacker of all. Upon viewing the human scalps hanging from Anderson's horse, the gentlemanly Price could barely contain his disgust at the psychopath Anderson. Price nevertheless offered Anderson the obligatory praise, claiming that if he only had 50,000 more men like Anderson, he could hold Missouri forever. For his part, Anderson greatly respected and admired Price, even presenting Price with a gift of two silver-mounted pistols at Boonville. (B. James George, Sr. Photograph Collection, State Historical Society of Missouri, public domain)

RIGHT
The teenage Jesse James, photographed near the time of Price's expedition. Sometime in spring 1864, the 16-year-old Jesse James had joined his older brother Frank in a guerrilla squad led by Fletcher Taylor. Frank himself had probably been part of Quantrill's band that had raided Lawrence in August 1863. (Photo by Underwood Archives/Getty Images)

The next day, September 25, Anderson's band disrupted telegraph lines between Hudson and Renick. By now Anderson, Todd, Poole, Cole the Younger, and several other bushwhacker chieftains were operating out of Boone and Audrain counties with about 400 men.

The Centralia Massacre, September 27

Early on September 27, Anderson led 80 guerrillas into nearby Centralia to drink and plunder, while over 200 bushwhackers remained three miles south of town. At 1130hrs a train pulled into Centralia. Among its passengers were 24 Federal soldiers on leave, unarmed but in uniform. All 24 soldiers were summarily shot and mutilated, save a single hostage.

Anderson's drunken and triumphant bushwhackers now rode out of town. They were shortly pursued by 147 troops of Major A.V.E. Johnson's 37th Missouri Volunteers. Anderson's guerrillas led the Missouri troops into yet another masterful trap and thoroughly massacred them, slaughtering 123 of Johnson's men and mutilating their bodies. Frank James later claimed his younger brother Jesse killed Major Johnson himself. In what proved Anderson's greatest and most grisly bushwhacker masterpiece, Missouri guerrillas had slaughtered an astonishing 146 Federal troops, while suffering just three dead and ten wounded.

On October 3, Federal militia burned Rocheport in retaliation for the town's perceived support of Anderson. Six days later, on October 9, Anderson and his men headed to Boonville to meet in person with Price.

THE RACE TO KANSAS, OCTOBER 8–21

Upon Price's invasion, Major General Rosecrans, commander of the Federal Department of Missouri, had urgently recalled Major General Alfred Pleasonton from leave back East. On October 8, Pleasonton arrived in Jefferson City, signaling a new stage of Federal military operations. Awaiting Pleasonton in the Missouri capital were 4,100 mounted troops. Acting with his usual decisiveness, Pleasonton re-organized these men into three provisional brigades, each led by one of Rosecrans' district commanders: Brigadier Generals Sanborn, Brown, and McNeil, all under the full command of Sanborn. Rosecrans ordered Sanborn's mounted force to chase after Price, keeping in contact with him, but also harassing and delaying Price's army as much as possible until more substantial Federal forces could be brought to bear.

Sanborn dispatched his 1st Brigade along the Springfield road towards the towns of Versailles and Warsaw, while sending the 2nd and 3rd Brigades down the railroad line to the towns of California and Tipton. By dawn on October 9, all three brigades had skirmished with the Fagan Division, then operating as Price's rearguard.

Confederate respite at Boonville, October 10–12

Price now turned the Army of Missouri northwest towards Boonville, a town of 3,000 well known for its strongly Confederate sympathies. The Army of Missouri reached Boonville on October 10, where it received a rapturous welcome from the local populace. About 1,200 to 1,500 local men and boys – mostly inexperienced and ill-equipped farmers – got caught up in the excitement and joined Price's army.

However, the Army of Missouri shortly wore out its welcome, as friendly provisioning soon developed into outright plunder. The new commander of Shelby's old Iron Brigade, Brigadier General M. Jeff Thompson, later wrote:

> What was done and not done here in the next three or four days I do not propose to relate, as I had only to try to control my own Brigade, to save their reputation from the demoralization which was seizing the army. The plunder of Boonville nearly completed this demoralization for many officers and men had loaded themselves, their horses and wagons with "their rights" and now wanted to turn Southwards and save what they had.

Meanwhile, despite being temporarily driven off by the Fagan Division, Sanborn had continued his dogged pursuit and harassment of the Army of Missouri until Price was finally compelled to employ both the Fagan

LEFT
Major General Alfred Pleasonton was the commander of the Army of the Potomac's Cavalry Corps, but was removed from command just before it started outperforming its Confederate counterpart. Pleasonton was the picture of the immaculately dressed cavalry officer. Pleasonton was notably ambitious and prone to self-promotion and public excuse-making. (Civil War photographs, 1861–1865, Library of Congress, Prints and Photographs Division)

RIGHT
Confederate Brigadier General Meriwether Jeff Thompson was named to command the Iron Brigade early in the Price expedition after its standing commander was killed in battle. Thompson had been a former member of the Missouri State Guard and was nicknamed the "Swamp Fox." (https://ehistory.osu.edu/books/battles/vol1/452, public domain, via Wikimedia Commons)

and Marmaduke Divisions – two-thirds of Price's army – to finally repulse Sanborn from the Boonville area on October 11. Sanborn withdrew to the south seeking provisions for his hungry men, finding four days' rations at the town of California and welcoming a fourth brigade, the 1,500 veteran cavalrymen of Colonel E.C. Catherwood. By October 13, Sanborn would again be headed back towards Boonville after Price.

Back at Boonville, Price ordered Anderson to "proceed to the north side of the Missouri River and permanently destroy the North Missouri Railroad, going as far east as practicable..." Price intended for Anderson to secure Price's flanks by denying the Federals the ability to move troops by rail. However, Price was unaware that Todd's and Anderson's summer raids across northern Missouri had already immobilized local rail traffic. Price also planned for Quantrill to raid the Hannibal & St. Joseph Railroad, but Quantrill would prove mysteriously absent.

By October 12, Price's Army of Missouri was still encamped in Boonville. However, Price had become increasingly aware of the Federal forces closing in against him from multiple sides. Price accordingly departed Boonville and marched for Chouteau Springs, 11 miles away. The Army of Missouri had always been too large for Boonville to support for any length of time, and for all their staunch pro-Confederate sympathies, after two days the people of Boonville were probably happy to see Price's men leave.

The battle of Glasgow, October 15

The evening of October 12, intelligence reached Price that a significant cache of military provisions, including a purported 5,000 small arms, lay in the nearby town of Glasgow. Price thus dispatched a combined force under Brigadier General John Clark to capture Glasgow and its supplies, while simultaneously sending a second force under Brigadier General M. Jeff Thompson against Sedalia.

Clark's force consisted of his own brigade from Marmaduke's Division, plus 500 men of Colonel Sidney D. Jackman's Brigade, of the Shelby Division. At 0500hrs on the morning of October 15, two pieces of Shelby's artillery, sited on the west bank of the Missouri, opened preparatory fire on the town of Glasgow and Colonel Chester Harding's 800 Federal defenders on the opposite side of the river. The joint attack was to have been coordinated, but Clark's combined brigade of 1,800 Confederate troops was delayed two hours in getting across the Missouri River. Eventually, however, they had rallied and were eventually advancing into Glasgow. The Confederates drove towards Harding's main defensive works on a hill commanding the town. The Federals leveled heavy small arms fire at the Confederates, who chose to dart between houses and fences, cautiously using cover and sharpshooters to advance towards the Federals rather than a costly frontal assault. The Confederates eventually closed under cover to within 30–50 yards of the Federal defenders.

Confederate Brigadier General John B. Clark, Jr. was 33 years old when he commanded the Clark Brigade during the Price expedition. Clark was the son of a three-term representative to Congress and after the Civil War he would himself serve as a Missouri Congressman for five terms. Clark died in 1903 at the age of 72. (John A. Scholten, public domain, via Wikimedia Commons)

After a fierce fight, but with no hope of repelling the inevitable final assault, Harding surrendered his 800 Federals to the Confederates, who allowed their prisoners to march out with full military honors. Glasgow was thus far the largest victory that Price's Army of Missouri had won in the field, and helped boost Confederate morale after the Fort Davidson disaster. Clark then headed towards the town of Marshall to rejoin Price's main army. Among the military spoils, the Confederates captured 1,200 rifles and 1,200 Federal overcoats, which were immediately distributed throughout the Army of Missouri.

Unfortunately, Glasgow's story does not end there. The previous day, October 14, Bloody Bill Anderson had dispatched 80 of his bushwhacker guerrillas east into Montgomery County. Anderson's men sacked Danville, killing several militiamen and civilians, plundered the stores, and burned most of the town down. They then continued east and burned the North Missouri Railroad depots at Florence and High Hill before fleeing back west ahead of local militia.

Meanwhile, after Clark and Jackman had left Glasgow, Anderson led a small band of bushwhackers into the town, where Anderson and his men extorted $5,000 from a prominent Glasgow citizen through torture, then allegedly mass-raped many black female slaves. Anderson then rendezvoused with his returning band of raiders. For his part, Quantrill also led a band into Glasgow and robbed $21,000 from the town bank. Afterwards, the ever mercurial Quantrill fled Glasgow and went into hiding, having mysteriously exited the campaign for good.

The battle of Sedalia, October 15

Price had likewise sent a second force of about 1,000 men and a section of artillery under Brigadier General Thompson to Sedalia "to attack the Federal force at that place should he deem it advisable and prudent." Sedalia held strategic value as a railroad terminus. Thompson's cavalry force moved quickly, and ten miles from its destination it spied a large Federal cavalry force headed west towards Lexington. Thompson's cavalry then picked off a few Federal stragglers who revealed that they were escorting Pleasonton on his way to join Sanborn. Friendly locals advised Thompson that Federal infantry was already on the nearby Lamine River. Thompson promptly fired off a dispatch, warning Price that Pleasonton might already be ahead of Price's main body. Thompson then used his fresh intelligence to slip through the separated Federal forces to attack Sedalia.

A small Federal garrison had indeed been left behind at Sedalia, where it defended two redoubts. After a brief clash on October 15, Thompson's troops routed the Federal defenders and took Sedalia, capturing about 200 men as well as "several hundred stand of arms, many pistols, and several wagon loads of goods suitable to soldiers," according to Price's report. Knowing superior Federal forces were nearby, Thompson departed Sedalia just a few hours after taking it. There was no time to either take the Federal prisoners along or even properly parole them in writing. As Thompson later explained, he simply gathered the Federal prisoners together and "made a 'spread eagle' speech. I paroled them verbally."

Under cover of darkness, Thompson's men again slipped past Pleasonton's superior Federal force, rendezvousing with Price's main army outside Waverly three days later on October 18. That same day, Clark also returned to the Army of Missouri from his foray against Glasgow. The two diversionary raids had been detached at the same time, with both successfully striking their objectives 60 miles apart, then returned simultaneously, both having won valuable provisions and intelligence at little cost. The combined double raid was hardly a noteworthy accomplishment in the grand scheme of Confederate cavalry operations, but for the Army of Missouri it was one of the campaign's more impressive performances, and was largely owed to the skill of Price's subordinates, Clark and Thompson.

The Federal pursuit through central Missouri

But time was running out for the Army of Missouri. Despite his often capable lieutenants, Price had marched at a leisurely pace, accomplishing relatively little, while his Federal counterparts had relentlessly driven their own units with the urgency of men watching their commands get invaded and their reputations gravely threatened. The Army of Missouri was slowly becoming surrounded by Federal forces. As Price marched west towards Kansas, he was doggedly pursued from the east by Pleasonton's Missouri provisional cavalry, and permanently hemmed in from the north by the uncrossable Missouri River.

Meanwhile, coming up from the southeast was Major General A.J. Smith's Federal infantry. Indeed, back on October 15, Rosecrans had used riverboats to move XVI Corps' 1st Division and Winslow's XVI Corps cavalry to Jefferson City, where the former would reinforce XVI Corps' 3rd Division. The previous day, Sanborn's cavalry had also renewed its westward pursuit of Price after a brief rest in the town of California. Winslow's XVI Corps cavalry was shortly attached to Sanborn. Now commanding four cavalry brigades, Sanborn marched through Georgetown up the Georgetown–Lexington road, reaching Crook's Store on the afternoon of October 15. From here, Sanborn made plans for "resisting the advance of the enemy, and attacking his flanks should he advance immediately."

Together, these separate Federal forces – Sanborn's and Winslow's cavalry, and the 1st and 3rd Divisions of XVI Corps – continued their pursuit of Price's Army of Missouri as all formations, Federal and Confederate, inevitably bore down on Kansas.

Rallying Curtis' Army of the Border

By October 1864, the state of Kansas, and in particular its standing government, had once again grown complacent regarding the American Civil War at large. Since 1862, the nearest large battles had taken place deep in Arkansas, while the controversial General Order No. 11 had largely pushed even guerrilla warfare out of Kansas after October 1863. Militarily, the most pressing concern was the ongoing Cheyenne War that had just erupted with the Plains Indians. However, the "Indian menace" largely only concerned those Kansans who lived on the frontier.

Major General Curtis, commander of the Department of Kansas, had first learned that Price had crossed the Arkansas River and might invade southern Kansas on September 13, while Curtis was encamped at the Solomon River overseeing operations against the Plains Indians.

Curtis immediately headed back to Fort Leavenworth, arriving on September 20. Curtis only had 7,000 troops throughout his entire Department of Kansas, comprising Kansas, Colorado, and Nebraska. Many of these were dispersed throughout the department's western frontier and would be impossible to recall in time to meet a potential invasion of Kansas by Price.

Curtis would have to rally what men and officers he could. First, Curtis sent a message to his South Kansas District commander, Major General James Blunt, to break off his pursuit mission and proceed as quickly as possible to Fort Leavenworth with as many troops as he could gather. Additionally, the 11th, 15th, and 16th Kansas Volunteer Cavalry regiments were already deployed along the Kansas–Missouri border, along with the 2nd Colorado Volunteer Cavalry and parts of the 3rd Wisconsin Volunteer Cavalry. These forces together combined to perhaps 4,000 troops. This was simply not enough to defend against a Confederate invasion. The only way to flesh out Curtis' defense of Kansas was to augment the volunteers with militia. That same day, September 20, Curtis fired off a telegram to Kansas Governor Thomas Carney, informing Carney of everything Curtis knew about the potential invasion, and warning Carney to prepare the Kansas militia "to be ready to cooperate against the foe." Carney remained skeptical, but in a September 21 correspondence agreed to help Curtis distribute weapons and equipment to much of the militia.

Governor Thomas Carney was the moderate Republican governor of Kansas in 1864 and arch-enemy of the state's Radical Republican faction led by Senator Jim Lane. Carney's paranoia at a potential Radical Republican conspiracy caused him to distrust capable generals such as Curtis and Blunt. (kansasmemory.org, Kansas State Historical Society)

The problem, as always, was the snake pit of Kansas politics. Kansas was dominated by the Republican Party, but it was a Republican Party convulsed by two opposing factions: moderate Republicans led by the sitting Governor Carney, and Radical Republicans who rallied behind the fiery Senator Jim Lane – the "Grim Chieftain" and infamous Jayhawker.

Facing Governor Carney in the November elections was Colonel Samuel J. Crawford, a Radical Republican of the Lane faction. Major General Curtis was an outspoken Crawford supporter, and Blunt even more so. To Carney, Curtis' September 17 recall of Blunt looked like a preliminary move to putting Blunt in command of the entire KSM. More importantly, Carney became increasingly paranoid that the supposed invasion crisis was a Radical Republican conspiracy to remove salt-of-the-earth moderate Republican voters – that is, farmers and militiamen – from the state during the scheduled November 8 elections.

Colonel Crawford had been nominated for governor on September 8 and would be awarded leave home on October 1. However, by Crawford's return to Kansas, he would learn of the Price invasion and immediately volunteer his services alongside Lane as a member of Curtis' staff, further stoking Carney's paranoia of a Radical Republican conspiracy.

Forced to await decisive action from Carney, Curtis busied himself by arming existing fieldworks along the eastern Kansas border, then constructing new ones to defend Olathe, Lawrence, Paola, and Fort Scott. Heavy siege guns were then placed at the most strategic of these locations.

Meanwhile, Price's actual location, never mind his intentions, remained unknown to Curtis. However, on September 29, Curtis would receive a telegram from Rosecrans reporting on the Fort Davidson battle and announcing that "the question of Price's being in Missouri is settled." Whether Price would subsequently invade Kansas remained unknown.

Unfortunately, Curtis' message recalling Blunt could not be read until Blunt returned to base. In late September, Blunt had led a column of 400 Federal cavalry out of Fort Larned in central Kansas on an Indian pursuit mission. For four days, Blunt's Federal cavalrymen had pursued a war party of 1,500 Cheyenne and Arapaho warriors north towards the Smoky Hill River, resulting in a fierce but indecisive four-hour battle at Pawnee Fork. The warriors had fled up the Pawnee River, and were chased for two straight days before Blunt recalled his exhausted force. As Blunt's column made its way back towards Fort Larned, it was intercepted by a courier bearing Curtis' message. Blunt relinquished his command to a subordinate and rode hard for Fort Leavenworth.

A Cheyenne scout seen in a late 19th-century painting. The Cheyenne War was a happy coincidence for Price, as it would distract and disorganize the already stretched thin Department of Kansas exactly when Kansas' meager Federal forces would be needed to defend against Price's invasion. (Henry Farny, public domain, via Wikimedia Commons)

Major General James G. Blunt was born in Maine in 1826 and became captain of his own merchant vessel by the age of 20. Upon returning ashore, Blunt became a physician and later became an abolitionist involved in Kansas politics and eventually a Union general. Blunt was always moody but he performed very well at Westport. (Civil War photographs, 1861–1865, Library of Congress, Prints and Photographs Division)

Blunt arrived late on October 8, picked up his close ally, Senator Jim Lane, and met with Curtis, who apprised Blunt and Lane of the situation. Curtis then ordered Blunt to Olathe to await further orders, while assigning his longtime friend Lane to his own headquarters staff with the rank of colonel.

As Price crossed into western Missouri the first week of October, the Federal Departments of Missouri and Kansas fired telegram after telegram to each other. Curtis had by now grown frantic to enlist Carney's support. Late on October 8, Carney told Curtis he would call up the militia. Yet Carney wavered again the following day, October 9, directly wiring Rosecrans in St. Louis: "Are we in danger here from Price? Inform me." By 1700hrs, Rosecrans had responded quite strongly in the affirmative that Price was just 15 miles below Jefferson City and would soon be "plundering Kansas."

On the evening of October 9, Governor Carney finally admitted the threat to Kansas was real. He agreed to mobilize the KSM under the condition that the militia would largely take over garrisoning duties in order to free the volunteer troops for active operations against Price's invading army. Command of the KSM would fall to Major General George Deitzler, who established his headquarters in Olathe.

For all of Governor Carney's earlier reluctance, his October 9 proclamation to the Kansas militia proved stirring stuff:

> Kansans, rally! You will do so, as you have always promptly done when your soil has been invaded. The call this time will come to you louder and stronger because you know the foe will seek to glut his vengeance upon you. Meet him, then, at the threshold and strike boldly; strike as one man against him. Let all business be suspended. The work to be done now is to protect the State against the marauder and murderer. Until this is accomplished we must lead a soldier's life and do a soldier's duty. Men of Kansas, rally! One blow, one earnest, united blow will foil the invader and save you. Who will falter? Who is not ready to meet the peril? Who will not defend his home and the State? To arms then! To arms, and the tended field until the rebel foe shall be baffled and beaten back!

The following day, October 10, Major General Curtis declared martial law. All able-bodied Kansas men between the ages of 18 and 60 were required to report for emergency military service. The Kansas militia were to rally at Shawnee Town. By October 11, some 3,300 Kansas militiamen were on the march towards Leavenworth. The following morning another 1,000 militia from Douglas County assembled in Lawrence. By evening, they had been reinforced by 800 militia from Jefferson County and 700 from Shawnee County.

Blunt had arrived in Olathe back on October 10, where he received orders to relieve Major General George Sykes of command of the District of South Kansas. Blunt did so, established his headquarters at Paola, and began organizing his few troops.

The Kansas troops continued to marshal, and on October 13, Major General Curtis designated his new force the Army of the Border. Its left wing comprised the KSM, commanded by Major General George Deitzler, while its right wing would be Major General Blunt's force, designated the Provisional

Cavalry Division. That same day Blunt received orders to depart for Hickman Mills, Missouri, which he reached on October 14. On October 15, Blunt was significantly reinforced by the arrival of the veteran 15th and 14th Kansas Volunteer Cavalry regiments under the command of Colonel Charles R. "Doc" Jennison and Colonel Charles W. Blair, respectively, as well as substantial Kansas infantry militia under Brigadier General William H.M. Fishback and Colonel James D. Snoddy.

Shortly before Blunt's advance to Hickman Mills, Curtis had dispatched Colonel James H. Ford's 2nd Colorado Cavalry on a scouting mission towards Independence, Missouri. It soon became clear that Price was headed that way; the population was pro-Southern and had been advised to preserve any possible forage. Ford left two companies in Independence as forward outposts and then withdrew south to Hickman Mills to join Blunt.

Blunt meanwhile had organized his Provisional Cavalry Division into three brigades. These were the 1st Brigade commanded by Colonel Charles R. "Doc" Jennison of the 15th Kansas Cavalry, the 2nd Brigade commanded by Colonel Thomas Moonlight of the 11th Kansas Cavalry, and the 3rd Brigade under Colonel Charles W. Blair of the 14th Kansas Cavalry. However, subordinated within Colonel Blair's 3rd Brigade were the militia forces of Brigadier General William H.M. Fishback, producing an awkward command situation.

By October 15, a total of 17,000 Kansas men had reported for service, and 15,000 of these were deployed along the Kansas–Missouri state line to await the Confederate invasion. However, it had been a full week since Governor Carney's order to mobilize, and no further news of Price had been heard. Both men and officers had become increasingly disenchanted.

On October 16, Mound City's Lieutenant Colonel James D. Snoddy, commanding the 6th KSM, requested permission from Blunt to take his men back home to Linn County. Blunt refused. Snoddy turned back home anyway, forcing Blunt to personally arrest both Snoddy and his immediate superior, Brigadier General Fishback. The 6th KSM promptly elected veteran Jayhawker Colonel James Montgomery its new commander. Blunt noted that no other officers or men of the Kansas militia regiments had rejected his authority, while regretting that political considerations prevented him from simply executing Snoddy and Fishback as was standard military practice. Nevertheless, pro-Carney Kansas newspapers continued publishing editorials claiming Price had departed Missouri and returned south, and requested the militiamen be released. Some regiments opposed crossing deep into Missouri, while others refused to cross the state line at all. Even Deitzler believed Price had already crossed the Arkansas River well to the south. By October 20, the situation had become so critical that the provost-marshal-general at Fort Leavenworth urged Curtis to suspend the "highly treasonable" *Leavenworth Times* and see its "editors and writers arrested as enemies to the public and cause" adding that its "incendiary articles are the cause mainly of the tendency to bad conduct of the militia ... please instruct."

However, that same day Curtis received a telegram from Rosecrans informing him that Price had been sighted at Waverly, Missouri, four days earlier, on October 16, and that Rosecrans' forces were beginning to pursue Price. Rosecrans described his own forces' disposition, then noted, "combined with yours, it seems to me we can push the old fellow [Price] and make him lose his train. His horses' feet must be

Colonel James Montgomery was a radical abolitionist and one of the original Kansas Jayhawkers. Like his partner-in-crime Jennison, the Federal authorities at one point transferred Montgomery out of Kansas to keep him more under control. Montgomery commanded the 2nd South Carolina Colored Volunteers in 1863 before eventually returning to Kansas in time for Westport. (Leonard & Martin, public domain, via Wikimedia Commons)

in bad order for want of shoes." Curtis then saw to it that the telegram was published in Kansas newspapers to convince skeptical militiamen and citizens that the danger of a Confederate invasion of Kansas was real. However, by now news had also arrived of Price's assault on Lexington.

The battle of Lexington, October 19

At 1900hrs on October 16, Blunt's 1st and 2nd Brigades, totaling 2,000 Federal cavalry and eight mountain howitzers, marched out of Hickman Mills, Missouri, towards Holden. Along the way they absorbed Major Emory S. Foster's battalion of irregular Missouri cavalry.

By 1000hrs, October 18, Major General Blunt's 2,000 cavalry had occupied Lexington, Missouri, a town of 4,122 people some 40 miles east of Kansas City. Upon reaching Lexington, Blunt was informed that Price had occupied Waverly, just 20 miles to the east. Additional information was received informing Blunt that Sanborn had only reached Crook's Store well to the southeast, meaning Sanborn was still too distant for Blunt to coordinate with against Price. In fact Sanborn was actually much further away, at Blackwater. More bad news was received that day in a message from Curtis, Blunt later recalling "that in consequence of the embarrassments thrown in his way by the Governor of Kansas and others relative to moving the militia out of the State, no reinforcements could be sent to me." Blunt's only real option was to stand fast at Lexington against Price's Army of Missouri and buy as much time as possible for Federal forces from Rosecrans' Department of Missouri to close within striking range of Price.

A modern-day view of the Lafayette County Courthouse in Lexington, Missouri. According to the US Census, Lexington had an 1860 population of 4,122. The town had been the site of an earlier battle when it was occupied by Sterling Price and his Missouri State Guard in 1861. (Simon Montgomery/ Alamy Stock Photo)

Price's Army of Missouri had reached the town of Marshall on October 15, whereupon Price had chosen to temporarily halt until he could be rejoined by Clark's and Thompson's Brigades. However, Price had become increasingly aware the Federals were attempting to trap his army in between Sanborn's pursuing forces and the KSM, whom he was informed were marching east to intercept him. On October 19, the Army of Missouri departed Marshall, resuming its march west towards Kansas in three division columns. At 1400hrs that day, Shelby's Division collided with Blunt's forward picket line a mile outside Lexington. Price was marching up from the south and thus ran into Colonel Moonlight's 2nd Brigade, which had established company-sized pickets blocking the Warrensburg and Dover roads.

Blunt was severely outnumbered, having just 2,000 men and eight mountain howitzers with which to defend Lexington. But Blunt's troops put up a fierce delaying action for several hours, only finally giving ground after Price committed Fagan's and Marmaduke's Divisions to the assault. Price later acknowledged the Federals "fought well and resisted strenuously" while believing that he was in fact facing 3,000 to 4,000 Federal troops. Blunt eventually ordered a withdrawal that evening, having succeeded in his goal "to develop his [Price's] force and movements and accomplish the object of a reconnaissance." Blunt's retreat was covered by Colonel Moonlight's partly dismounted 2nd Brigade. As the sky grew darker, Price's men drove the Federals out of Lexington and down the road towards Independence. With nightfall, Price ordered a halt to the pursuit, allowing Moonlight's hard-pressed 2nd Brigade to escape intact. Price's Army of Missouri went into camp.

Blunt's cavalry force continued to retreat from Lexington until 0200hrs on October 20, stopping east of the Little Blue River. Blunt fully expected to mount another stand, and ordered that ammunition and reinforcements be sent forward to him at the Little Blue River, which he reached six hours later at 0800hrs.

The campaign was about to reach its climax. Even back East, Price's expedition had become a matter of concern. Lieutenant General Ulysses S. Grant, general-in-chief of all Federal armies in the field, and no fan of Rosecrans, messaged his chief-of-staff Major General Henry Halleck: "Has Rosecrans yet come upon Price? If he has not he should be removed at once. Price is in a country where he supports his army without difficulty, and there is no reason why our forces should not move without delay ... Anybody ... will be better than Rosecrans."

Rosecrans' Army of the Department of Missouri, October 19–21

Rosecrans had recalled Major General Pleasonton from his Pennsylvania leave early, naming Pleasonton the department's field commander in the pursuit of Price. Pleasonton had reached St. Louis on October 6. By October 19, Pleasonton had caught up with the Department of Missouri's Provisional Cavalry Division at Dunksburg, Missouri. Taking command, Pleasonton re-organized the division into four brigades: the 1st Brigade under Brigadier General Egbert Brown, the 2nd Brigade under Brigadier General John McNeil, the 3rd Brigade under Brigadier General John B. Sanborn, and the 4th Brigade under XVI Corps' Colonel Edward F. Winslow. To each brigade Pleasonton attached an artillery section. The Missouri Provisional Cavalry Division, now commanded by Pleasonton and numbering about 7,000 troops, resumed its pursuit of Price. By nightfall on October 20, Pleasonton's lead units had encamped ten miles east of Lexington.

Additionally, Major General A.J. Smith's Federal XVI Corps, the campaign's only large regular infantry formation, was also moving up from the southeast. After marching 17 miles on October 20, through the autumn snow no less, Smith's XVI Corps bivouacked 23 miles short of Lexington. The XVI Corps, accompanied by Rosecrans, would arrive at Lexington the following day, October 21. However, Rosecrans was worried that Price's Army of Missouri might slip past Curtis' right wing, and so he immediately sent Smith's weary XVI Corps marching south towards the town of Chapel Hill, with the ultimate objective of Lone Jack. From here XVI Corps would be in a blocking position against any Price end run to the south.

The battle of the Little Blue River, October 21

Late on October 20, a concerned Major General Curtis dispatched an urgent message to Blunt ordering him to leave a token rearguard at the Little Blue and instead fall back towards Independence, seven miles to the west. However, by 2200hrs the increasingly confident Blunt messaged back to Curtis, "Here is the place to make the fight" and even urged Curtis to come forward personally and form his own assessment of the Little Blue River's tactical advantages.

Brigadier General John B. Sanborn commanded the District of Southwest Missouri and later Pleasonton's 3rd Brigade. Sanborn would directly command Pleasonton's cavalry during the October 25 battle of the Marais des Cygnes, performing somewhat poorly. (Photo by Hulton Archive/ Getty Images)

However, Curtis remained hamstrung by Governor Carney, who refused to allow the KSM to march east of the Big Blue River. Curtis reiterated his instructions to Blunt, who chose to leave a detachment of Colonel Moonlight's 2nd Brigade as a rearguard on the west bank of the Little Blue River, while Blunt's main force fell back towards Independence, as ordered, late on the night of October 20.

Behind them Colonel Moonlight's delaying force at the Little Blue River consisted only of the 11th Kansas Cavalry and a mountain howitzer battery. They worked feverishly to build improvised fieldworks along roads and river fords and were ready to fight by dawn, October 21. Moonlight put Major Martin Anderson in command of two companies and the mountain howitzer battery anchoring the covered bridge on the Lexington–Independence road. One mile to the north, Captain James Greer's I Company defended a river ford, while the ford one mile to the south was defended by Captain Joel Huntoon's H Company. Moonlight placed a small skirmish line one mile ahead, while Moonlight's remaining companies formed a reserve on higher ground to the west.

Meanwhile, Price's Army of Missouri had departed Lexington on October 20 and begun marching towards Independence, making 20 miles by nightfall. The following morning, October 21, saw Brigadier General Clark's Brigade in the vanguard of Price's army. Clark's Confederates ran into Moonlight's skirmish line at 0700hrs and drove them over the Little Blue River bridge a mile to the west. Clark rallied his forces in an attempt to capture the bridge, while also sending detachments to the north and south to find possible crossings. The 11th Kansas drenched the Confederate attack in heavy fire, delaying Clark's advance. Meanwhile, once the Federal skirmishers were safely back across the river, Major Anderson ordered a wagon full of burning hay be pushed into the bridge, successfully destroying the bridge by 1000hrs. However, while the main action at the bridge was taking place, Colonel Lawther's 10th Confederate Missouri reported finding a viable crossing, downstream to the north of the bridge. Even as the bridge burned, Clark shifted most of his brigade to the north crossing. Moonlight recognized the danger and ordered the majority of his force to withdraw and establish a new defensive line near the Lawson Moore House, on the high ground to the north. Moonlight realized the Confederate advance by Lawther's 10th Missouri was unsupported and ordered an aggressive counterattack against the budding Confederate bridgehead.

The Confederate 10th Missouri, now on the far side of the river, was compelled to attack uphill towards the Lawson Moore House to clear the Federal defenses. Likewise Clark was forced to commit his arriving regiments to the battle piecemeal in an attempt to support the 10th Missouri. Repeated Confederate attacks against the Federal high ground were absorbed and eventually repelled by Moonlight's Kansans, who chased them back down the slopes. The combat was particularly fierce, with soldiers firing at each other from as little as 30 yards. A Confederate private reported, "The Union boys … came out from their well-concealed positions and fought us on the blue grass ridges but with little protection … both sides fought like demons." Marmaduke himself would have two horses shot out from underneath him during the action. Marmaduke urgently messaged Price to send Shelby's Division as reinforcements. Moonlight shortly spied Shelby's Division moving up in support of Marmaduke. By now, the rest of Blunt's Division was visible marching towards the battle from Independence. Moonlight decided he had accomplished his mission to delay Price and ordered his force to fall back and link up with the advancing Blunt at the Little Blue Church.

By 1100hrs, Blunt had formed his reunited division of 2,800 men, including Moonlight's 2nd Brigade, along the ridge overlooking the Little Blue River. From here Blunt saw Shelby's Division overtaking the Marmaduke Division. Blunt quickly seized the opportunity to hit Shelby's temporarily unsupported lead brigade. The Federals attacked and drove Shelby's Confederates back half a mile, while the exhausted Marmaduke Division did little to help. Fighting dismounted, Blunt had about 2,100 troopers firing into the advancing Confederates, with the remaining 700 (every fourth man) in the rear holding four horses each.

Born in Forfarshire, Scotland, in 1833, Colonel Thomas Moonlight of the 11th Kansas Cavalry commanded Blunt's 2nd Brigade cavalry and would later serve as a Kansas Supreme Court Justice and eventually be appointed the governor of Wyoming Territory. (Library of Congress, public domain, via Wikimedia Commons)

However, Shelby's larger division of 3,000 men, with perhaps 200 additional troops from Marmaduke's, slowly closed and flanked Blunt's outnumbered forces. Shortly after 1200hrs, Blunt began gradually pulling his attacking troops back to the ridge. After re-establishing the high defensive line near the Salem Church, Blunt's outnumbered division, with its 15 field guns, poured heavy artillery fire onto Thompson's Brigade of the Shelby Division, which had been advancing uphill towards the church before stalling in the face of Blunt's firepower. Shelby then sent Colonel Jackman's Brigade on a flanking mission around Blunt.

It was at 1300hrs that Curtis suddenly appeared and unilaterally shifted Captain W.D. McLain's battery and two mountain howitzers to meet Jackman's flank attack. However, Curtis' sudden move weakened Federal artillery fire in the center and soon Shelby's troops were advancing in the center as well. By 1400hrs, Curtis and Blunt agreed on a difficult fighting withdrawal to Independence, which Blunt's Division reached at 1600hrs. It was soon apparent no immediate follow-on attack was imminent, and at 1700hrs Blunt ordered most of his division to withdraw from Independence and march for Curtis' main defensive line on the Big Blue River. Blunt left Lieutenant Colonel Samuel Walker's 16th Kansas Cavalry behind in Independence as a temporary delaying force while Moonlight's 11th Kansas Cavalry replenished its ammunition.

The battle of Independence, October 21

That evening Shelby's vanguard attacked Independence. Walker's 16th Kansas Cavalry, their ammunition exhausted, was forced to fall back. They ran into Moonlight's resupplied 11th Kansas Cavalry, which engaged Shelby's Confederates in a swirling mounted melee. The Kansans slowly gave ground through Independence, getting pushed out of town, but fighting fiercely until total darkness ended the action. Price's main army then occupied Independence as Moonlight's 11th Kansas Cavalry withdrew to reinforce Curtis' Big Blue defensive line by midnight.

Although smarting from Curtis' untimely interference that afternoon, Blunt's delaying action at the Little Blue River and Independence had helped buy time for Rosecrans' Army of the Department of Missouri to close the distance with Price. Indeed, that evening Pleasonton's Provisional Cavalry Division of 7,000 men made camp six miles east of the Little Blue River.

SHELBY'S DIVISION ADVANCES INTO INDEPENDENCE, OCTOBER 21 (PP.58–59)

Major General Blunt's roughly 3,000 Kansas cavalrymen had been defending the Little Blue River for most of October 21 when superior numbers and their own low ammunition forced the Kansans to conduct a fighting retreat to Independence. By 1600hrs, Blunt's rearguard had set up a defensive line on the eastern edge of the town. However, an hour later, Blunt ordered most of his cavalry to withdraw from Independence and march six miles west to Curtis' main defensive line on the Big Blue River. Lieutenant Colonel Samuel Walker's 16th Kansas Volunteer Cavalry remained in Independence to delay Price's advancing troops, while Colonel Thomas Moonlight's 11th Kansas Volunteer Cavalry remained outside Independence, replenishing ammunition.

That evening, Shelby's vanguard, as well as men from Marmaduke's Freeman Brigade, pushed warily into Independence and engaged Walker's 16th Kansas Cavalry. Before long, Walker's troops had exhausted their ammunition and were forced to fall back. They ran into Colonel Moonlight's resupplied unit, which engaged Shelby's Confederates **(1)** in a swirling mounted melee. The Kansans **(2)** slowly gave ground through Independence, with dismounted skirmishing continuing in the streets as dusk fell.

Eventually, Shelby's men pushed Moonlight's cavalry completely out of town, although fierce fighting continued until total darkness ended the action. Moonlight and his troops then retired west to rejoin Curtis at the Big Blue River.

Price plans for battle, late October 21

That same night, Price's Army of Missouri bivouacked within and outside Independence, with Pleasonton's cavalry just 13 miles to the east. Price was also well aware that Curtis' main force awaited him in a defensive line along the Big Blue River, just six miles to the west. Price used the next several hours to formulate his plan of attack.

Exactly what Price wished to accomplish – that is, his intentions – have never been exactly known. One option was to simply hold Curtis' Army of the Border north of Brush Creek, and Pleasonton's Provisional Cavalry Division east of the Big Blue River, and buy time for Price's army to slip into Kansas. A second, more aggressive option was to exploit interior lines of communication to defeat the immediate Federal threats in detail: to hold Pleasonton long enough to knock out Curtis in front of him, and then turn and defeat Pleasonton and escape before A.J. Smith's XVI Corps arrived. A third possible option, one supported by Price biographer Albert Castel, is that Price was as yet unsure and wished to see how events would develop.

The battle ensign of Colonel Thomas Moonlight's 11th Kansas Volunteer Cavalry as preserved by the Kansas State Historical Society in Topeka. The 11th Kansas Cavalry was formed in April 1863 from the 11th Kansas Infantry and served the entire war under Colonel Moonlight. (Kansas State Historical Society)

If Price's overall intent is unclear, the disposition and missions of his forces are not. Shelby's Division was in the vanguard, and would spearhead the assault. Price directed Shelby's Division to feint against the main crossing on the Independence–Kansas City road, then force the true crossing farther to the south, beyond Brush Creek. Following behind Shelby would be Fagan's Division, which would escort Price's swollen, ponderous wagon train as it trundled southwest down the Santa Fe road towards New Santa Fe. Finally, the Marmaduke Division would make up Price's rearguard, with the mission of holding up Pleasonton's Provisional Cavalry Division coming up from the east.

THE BATTLE OF WESTPORT, OCTOBER 22–23

Curtis' combined force of volunteers and Kansas militia remained about 15,000. Just to the east, Pleasonton commanded about 7,500 cavalry, giving the Federals about 22,500 troops converging on Westport. Casualties and desertions had reduced Price to about 8,000 mounted troops, ensuring the Federals a 2.5:1 numerical advantage over the Confederates. The combined 30,500 troops would make the October 22–23 battle of Westport the largest battle ever fought west of the Mississippi River.

October 22 would open with two geographically separated actions. In the west, Curtis' and Blunt's Kansans – the Army of the Border – would defend the west bank of the Big Blue River against Price's inevitable attempt to cross. Six miles to the east, at Independence, Pleasonton's Provisional Cavalry Division of the Department of Missouri would attack Price's rearguard in hopes of eventually linking up with Curtis and crushing Price in between them.

The battle of Independence, October 22

Curtis had intended Blunt's October 21 delaying action at the Little Blue to buy time not just for Curtis to fortify his main defensive line on the Big Blue River, but also for Pleasonton and Smith to close the distance with Price. Pleasonton's pursuit of Price had thus far been somewhat slow, although ironically Pleasonton later claimed that *he* was trying to give *Curtis* time to prepare his fortifications. Regardless, Curtis felt secure in his defensive lines, making it vital that Pleasonton and Smith be implored to hurry the pursuit. However, as of October 21, Curtis was in contact with Rosecrans, but had not heard from either Pleasonton or Smith since before October 19. Therefore, late on October 21, Curtis dispatched veteran scout Daniel Boutwell of the 2nd KSM to sneak through Confederate lines and make contact with Pleasonton. Meanwhile, by 0500hrs on October 22, Pleasonton's Provisional Cavalry Division had reached the Little Blue River. Several hours later an intrepid Boutwell was relaying his message to Pleasonton that Curtis' army was just 13 miles to the west.

Suddenly inspired, Pleasonton swung into action. Pleasonton's men quickly crossed the Little Blue by constructing a makeshift bridge to replace the one Moonlight had burned the previous day. The October 22 battle of Independence would see Pleasonton's 7,000 Federal cavalry attacking Price's rearguard, the 4,500-strong Marmaduke Division. Another 2,500 troops of Fagan's Division, in the center of Price's column, would become engaged as reinforcements.

In Pleasonton's vanguard was Brigadier General McNeil's 2nd Brigade, comprising Colonel E.C. Catherwood's 13th Missouri Cavalry and Colonel J.L. Beveridge's 17th Illinois Cavalry. These two regiments shortly ran into Price's rearguard – Cabell's and Slemons' Brigades of the Fagan Division. Cabell and Slemons had deployed in a defensive line outside Independence, and were supported by Captain W.M. Hughey's Arkansas Confederate Battery of Parrott guns. McNeil's brigades nevertheless slowly forced Fagan's troops back. As the Confederates neared Independence, their resistance became stiffer and McNeil requested reinforcements. These arrived in the form of Sanborn's 3rd Brigade and Major F.M. Malone's battle-tested 7th Kansas Cavalry.

By 1330hrs, Pleasonton's cavalry had advanced three of the seven miles towards Independence. An hour and a half later, the Federals were pushing into the town's eastern outskirts. McNeil and Sanborn prepared a decisive

The modern-day Community of Christ Temple in Independence, Missouri. Part of the October 22, 1864 battle of Independence was fought on the modern-day Temple Lot. The nautilus-shaped Temple itself was completed in 1994. (Ecjmartin1, public domain, via Wikimedia Commons)

LEFT
The battle ensign of the 7th Kansas Volunteer Cavalry as preserved by the Kansas State Historical Society. The 7th Kansas Cavalry had been established by Charles "Doc" Jennison in October 1861 and were the original "Jennison's Jayhawkers." (Kansas State Historical Society)

RIGHT
Missouri bushwhacker leader, Lieutenant George Todd. Todd had been with Quantrill's Raiders during the October 1863 Baxter Springs Massacre when Curtis' son had been killed. The news that Todd had himself been killed on October 22 caused Curtis to write a letter to his wife that night informing her that their son had been partially avenged. (John N. (John Newman) Edwards, public domain, via Wikimedia Commons)

cavalry attack. A concentrated column of companies roared through town, sabers drawn. The 13th Missouri Cavalry, 7th Kansas Cavalry, and 17th Illinois Cavalry struck from the east, while the 2nd Arkansas Cavalry hit the Confederates in the flank from the northeast. The Arkansan-versus-Arkansan contest was naturally bitter and fierce, but the Unionists won decisively. The Federal Arkansans captured 300 of their Confederate Arkansan counterparts, and nearly captured Cabell as well.

While McNeil's and Sanborn's 2nd and 3rd Brigades secured Independence, Pleasonton sent Brown's 1st and Winslow's 4th Brigades through the town to pursue the fleeing Confederates. As darkness fell, Brown's 1st Brigade rode west down the Independence–Westport road and fell upon the withdrawing Confederate rearguard. Brown pushed the Confederates for two miles before retiring to Independence for ammunition.

Winslow's 4th Brigade took over the pursuit. A detachment of the 10th Missouri Union Cavalry under Lieutenant Colonel Frederick W. Benteen soon discovered the Confederates in the dark and signaled the 3rd Iowa Cavalry to attack. The result was a rare occurrence for the American Civil War: a pitched night action. By 2230hrs, October 22, Winslow's 4th Brigade had driven the Confederate cavalry to within three miles of Byram's Ford on the Big Blue River. However, Price's wagon train had already successfully crossed the river. Shortly afterwards the rest of Clark's force had also crossed, with the exception of its extreme rearguard, the 8th Confederate Missouri Cavalry. The Confederates had lost about 40 killed and almost 400 captured. Federal losses are strangely unknown, but McNeil's Brigade suffered the heaviest.

Among the day's Confederate casualties was Lieutenant George Todd. The bushwhacker chieftain had been leading a band of scouts two miles northeast of Independence when a Federal sniper shot him through the throat. Todd died a few hours later.

More critically, that same day, Pleasonton sent a fateful message to Rosecrans, requesting that Smith's XVI Corps infantry, marching south, be recalled to support his own troops. The hard-pressed XVI Corps would just miss trapping Price on their march south, then miss fighting Price altogether on their forced countermarch back. The decision may have proved the difference between the Federals merely repulsing Price's Army of Missouri in the field outside Westport, or possibly annihilating it entirely.

The battle of the Big Blue River, October 22

By the morning of October 22, Curtis had about 15,000 Federal troops – both volunteer and militia – assembled along the Big Blue River just east

Another Samuel J. Reader sketch, this time of a Kansas militia flag. The Kansas militiamen were poorly trained and, aside from their rifles, not terribly well equipped, but they provided the numbers badly needed to repel a Confederate invasion of Kansas. (kansasmemory.org, Kansas State Historical Society)

of Kansas City. The Federal defensive line, which Curtis had begun fortifying on October 15, began at the Big Blue's mouth on the Missouri River's southern bank, then stretched south along the Big Blue 15 miles to Russell's Ford near Hickman Mills. The main Federal entrenchments were on the Big Blue's steeper and more thickly vegetated western bank. Federal troops had additionally set up obstacles and dammed likely crossing points. Throughout October 21, under the urgent direction of Deitzler and Governor Carney, increasing numbers of Kansas militia had flowed into the entrenchments along the Big Blue River.

Curtis was convinced Price would cross the Big Blue River at its main ford and then march into Kansas by the most obvious route, a frontal assault straight down the Independence–Kansas City road. Curtis thus set up his Army of the Border headquarters where the Independence–Kansas City road crossed the Big Blue's main ford.

The Army of the Border's left (north) wing, straddling the Independence–Kansas City road, therefore comprised Curtis' main strength, boasting over 10,000 troops. These included the main KSM force of over 9,000 militiamen, plus Colonel Blair's 3rd Brigade, temporarily detached from Blunt's Provisional Cavalry Division. Commanding this north wing was the KSM's Major General Deitzler.

The night of October 21, Curtis had wired Rosecrans: "I am confident I can stop Price at this crossing [the Independence–Kansas City road] and hope you will come up in his rear and left so he cannot get out by Hickman Mills. If you can get that position we bag Price … my troops are in good order, and ready to make a stand at this place."

However, Curtis' subordinate, Blunt, vehemently disagreed, believing that Price would not be so foolish as to make a frontal assault down the Independence–Kansas City road against Curtis' main strength. Blunt insisted Price would only feint against the main Federal line, then slip off to the south and cross one of the upper forks. Events would prove Blunt correct, but Curtis ignored him.

Instead, Blunt would command the Federal right wing defending Curtis' southern flank. Blunt's force, once deployed, would comprise 4,500 troops, extending nine miles from the main ford south to Russell's Ford. However, Blunt's scrambling forces would not fully get into position until the morning of October 22.

Blunt's northernmost unit, the 900 men of Colonel Ford's 4th Brigade, defended the Independence–Westport road. Two miles to the south, Colonel Moonlight's 1,000-man 2nd Brigade defended Simmons' Ford about four miles directly east of Westport. Another four miles farther south, the 1,200 troops of Jennison's 1st Brigade protected Byram's Ford. Finally, on the far right of Curtis' line, to the far south, Brigadier General Melvin Grant commanded a notional brigade of 1,200 Kansas militiamen defending Russell's Ford, about four miles north of Hickman Mills, Missouri.

Price opened battle at 0900hrs on October 22. Confederate tactical command largely fell to Shelby, who advanced Colonel Sidney Jackman's brigade towards the main crossing of the Big Blue River; this was Price's planned feint. Jackman's Confederates shortly encountered Curtis' pickets and sent the Federal skirmishers scurrying back across the river. Seeing the Confederates' expected frontal assault, Curtis responded by sending Colonel Ford's 4th Brigade in a counterattack.

After about 30 minutes of fighting, Curtis began to grow alarmed at the Confederates' seemingly half-hearted attempts to advance. Only then, with a sudden shock of horror, did Curtis realize that the action in front of him was merely a feint – Price's main crossing would be attempted upriver to the south, around and through Curtis' weak right flank, exactly as Blunt had predicted the previous night.

Curtis dispatched a frantic message to Brigadier General Melvin Grant, commanding the 1,200 KSM at Russell's Ford on Curtis' extreme right wing: "Price is making very feeble demonstrations in front. Look out for your position. Send scouts out on road towards Pleasant Hill, and also towards Independence, to see if he [Price] is moving on my flank. Send me report every 30 minutes." Curtis additionally dispatched two aides to warn Blunt of the development, before moving his own headquarters west until reaching the intersection of the Hickman Mills road, allowing Curtis a better view of the entire Big Blue line.

By now Shelby had taken his old unit, Thompson's Iron Brigade, and begun probing Curtis' right wing for potential crossing points. After two hours, no easy crossings could be found and around 1100hrs, Shelby resigned himself to forcing a crossing at Byram's Ford.

The previous night, the 4th KSM had urgently blocked the Byram's Ford crossing with felled trees and other obstructions. By 0900hrs, October 22, Colonel Jennison's 1st Brigade had arrived at Byram's Ford to resist any Confederate crossing attempt there. Jennison immediately deployed mounted scouts on the Big Blue's east bank. High above the steep west bank, immediately above the ford itself, Jennison sited Lieutenant H.L. Barker's five howitzers, protected by skirmishers. Arrayed in depth behind the guns

Major General George Deitzler, adjutant general of Kansas and commander of the KSM. A vigorous Free Stater, Deitzler had served as an officer for the Free State forces during the 1855 Wakarusa War and served in Kansas' Free State legislature. In 1860, Deitzler was elected mayor of Lawrence and later became treasurer at the University of Kansas. (Mouseion Archives/Alamy Stock Photo)

An illustration of the October 22, 1864 battle of the Big Blue River. The strongest section of Curtis' Big Blue defensive line was the northern six miles terminating at the Big Blue mouth, where an anchored steamboat was defended by 250 troops of Colonel A.C. Hogan's 19th Kansas Militia. (kansasmemory.org, Kansas State Historical Society)

The 15th Kansas Volunteer Cavalry ensign as preserved by the Kansas State Historical Society in Topeka. The 15th Kansas Cavalry had been established in the fall of 1863 under Doc Jennison. Although Jennison was later expelled from the US Army, the 15th Kansas Cavalry survived the war to fight in the Powder River campaign in the Indian Wars. (Kansas State Historical Society)

were the dismounted 15th Kansas Cavalry, 3rd Wisconsin Cavalry, and an assemblage of KSM.

Around 1100hrs, a dismounted detachment of Jackman's Brigade made contact with Jennison's advance scouts. Over the next three hours, Jackman's Confederates, supported by Thompson's Iron Brigade, would make repeated frontal attacks into the face of Jennison's firepower before being driven back.

By 1400hrs, Shelby became convinced Byram's Ford could not be forced by direct assault. While Jackman maintained frontal pressure, Shelby dispatched Colonel Frank Gordon's 5th Missouri Confederate Cavalry upstream to find a crossing and a cavalry battalion under Lieutenant Colonel Alonzo Slayback downstream.

Slayback shortly found the little-used Hinkle's Ford, which the Federals were unaware of and Blunt had left undefended. Slayback's exuberant cavalry quickly crossed the Big Blue and hit Jennison's stunned 1st Brigade in the flank. Jennison's men fell back in panicked retreat.

Earlier, upon hearing the sound of artillery fire, Blunt had ordered Colonel Moonlight's 2nd Brigade to abandon its defensive position at Simmons' Ford and head south to support Jennison. However, Moonlight arrived just as Jennison's men were fleeing. Moonlight immediately ordered his men to gallop to the state line at Westport and set up a defensive line to receive Jennison and his pursuing Confederates.

However, some of Jennison's men managed to temporarily regroup and extricate their artillery battery, before continuing a more composed fighting withdrawal in front of Slayback's advancing Confederate cavalry.

Earlier that morning, Brigadier General Melvin Grant, commanding the 1,200 KSM on Curtis' extreme right wing, had followed his orders from Curtis to dispatch extensive scouting parties to determine Price's whereabouts. In the process, Grant had lost adequate command and control of his brigade.

Shelby, unaware of Grant's situation, believed a strong Federal force lay to the south that threatened Price's supply train. Shelby therefore began pulling units from Jackman's Brigade, engaged against Jennison, and dispatched them south to clear the train's escape route.

Aware of the fighting at Byram's Ford, Grant had attempted to send units to support Jennison. After learning of Jennison being driven out of Byram's Ford, Grant ordered his KSM brigade to withdraw towards Westport. However, Grant's inexperienced units marched piecemeal and not as a cohesive force.

Colonel Veale's 2nd KSM of 300 Shawnee County amateurs and Captain Ross Burnes' single 24-pounder brass howitzer found themselves alone and heavily outnumbered at the Mockbee Farm. Unfortunately for the Kansans, Colonel Gordon's 5th Missouri Confederate Cavalry had by now been reinforced by Jackman with an additional regiment and battalion of Confederate cavalry. According to a Kansas sergeant: "The contest was about to commence between a brigade of soldiers, Shelby's men, the flower of the Confederate Western Army, and about 300 Militia, composed of lawyers, doctors, preachers, farmers, and others, some of whom had never fired a gun."

At 1500hrs, Shelby's augmented force of professional cavalrymen slammed into Veale's heavily outnumbered Kansas militiamen. For 45 minutes, the battle raged at the Mockbee Farm, the fiercest clash of the day. Twice Shelby's men attacked. Several times the Kansans' line broke but re-formed, driving off the Confederates.

Colonel Jackman then appeared on the field and took charge of the situation. The surprisingly poised and stubborn Kansas farmers and shopkeepers, fighting dismounted and outnumbered, had thus far scored two straight repulses over the Confederate regulars. There would not be a third. Jackman and Gordon rallied the full might of their Confederate cavalry and artillery, and ordered an organized charge.

The Confederates' thundering cavalry charge lasted just a few minutes. When it was over, the Kansans had lost 24 men killed, 24 wounded, 88 captured, and over 100 horses dead. All 20 Kansas artillerymen were either killed or captured, including Captain Burnes. However, the outmatched Kansans had killed 43 Confederates. Among those captured was 2nd Lieutenant Samuel James Reader, a 28-year-old Indianola paymaster. Reader, a lifelong and avid diarist, would ultimately provide historians perhaps the most detailed and extensive eyewitness documentation of the climactic October 22–25 battles.

Brigadier General Grant and additional KSM survivors escaped across the state line to Olathe, while remnants of the 2nd KSM reached Wyandotte that night. They would redeploy to Kansas City the next day.

Meanwhile, Brigadier General Thompson's pursuing Iron Brigade was finding its hands increasingly full with Jennison's 1st Brigade of Kansas cavalrymen. Refusing to panic, Jennison's Jayhawkers fell back in good order towards Westport and made the Confederates pay for their advance. Jennison's fighting withdrawal slowed the Iron Brigade enough that Jennison's 1st Brigade, on the state line a few miles south of Westport, was soon joined by Colonel Moonlight's 2nd Brigade. Together the two Kansas cavalry brigades rallied and began to push Thompson's Confederates back. Shortly before dusk, Thompson's Iron Brigade withdrew two miles to the welcome cover of some woods. Jennison's and Moonlight's battered and weary cavalry wisely chose not to follow. They held their lines until dark and then withdrew back to Westport.

Once Curtis learned that his right wing had been flanked at Byram's Ford, he ordered Deitzler with his left wing of the Army of the Border to withdraw towards Kansas City. In the process, Colonel A.C. Hogan's rearguard 19th KSM was attacked by 500 of Fagan's cavalry. Hogan's Kansans drove them off, killing 12 Confederates and capturing ten more. By evening, Deitzler had his Kansas militiamen redeployed in new entrenchments around Kansas City.

Evening, October 22

When Blunt rode to Westport that evening, he found Ford's 4th Brigade, which Blunt immediately ordered to the Kansas City defensive entrenchments, accompanied by McLain's Independent Colorado Battery. Blunt deployed the 16th Kansas Cavalry in picket lines south of Westport, while leaving the 2nd Colorado Cavalry within the town itself. Jennison's 1st Brigade bivouacked just north of Westport, while Moonlight's 2nd Brigade made camp just east of the Shawnee Mission.

Among the 2nd Kansas Militia's members was 2nd Lieutenant Samuel J. Reader, a 28-year-old paymaster from Indianola. Reader had been a prolific diarist since the age of eight and his daily journal entries and post-battle sketches and paintings would become among the most valuable and compelling primary documentation of the Westport battle. (kansasmemory.org, Kansas State Historical Society)

Here is Reader's sketch of the Mockbee Farm's stone barn. (kansasmemory.org, Kansas State Historical Society)

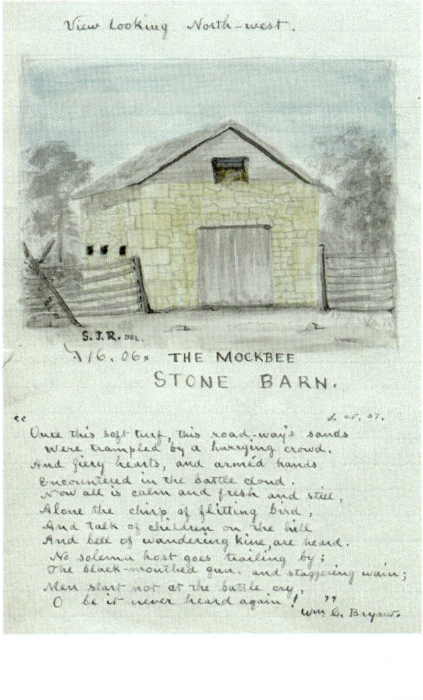

LAST STAND OF THE 2ND KANSAS STATE MILITIA AT MOCKBEE FARM, 1545HRS, OCTOBER 22 (PP.68–69)

At 1500hrs, Frank Gordon's 5th Missouri Confederate Cavalry, having crossed the Big Blue River at Byram's Ford, advanced south down a rural lane, directly into Captain Burnes' single brass 24-pounder gun **(1)** and its 21-man crew, who unlimbered in the lane alongside Mockbee Farm and opened fire directly into Gordon's skirmishers. Within minutes, Colonel Veale's 2nd KSM had arrived, dismounted, and assembled into a defensive line around Burnes' 24-pounder. The 2nd KSM and Burnes' gun shortly repulsed Gordon's men, inspiring Veale to advance a skirmish line 150 yards up the lane. A second, stronger Confederate attack came, comprising Gordon's 5th Missouri and some of the Jackman Brigade. Firing canister, the 24-pounder tore into the Confederate ranks, breaking the second attack.

The Kansas civilians had resisted so valiantly that Shelby believed he was facing Pleasonton's professional cavalry. Shelby ordered Thompson's Iron Brigade to break off its pursuit of Jennison and reinforce the Confederates. Before Thompson could arrive, Gordon and Jackman had fully rallied their units into their largest assault force yet, badly outnumbering the Kansan defenders. Finally, Shelby's third attack, larger and more organized, commenced on the Kansas militia.

According to Shelby's adjutant:

> The prairie shook… the trampled grass, cut and whirled into yellow dust, rose up in clouds of smoke … Not a shout, nor yell, nor battle-cry as the men **(2)** neared the blue spot, coiled and massed like a group of rattlesnakes **(3)**. Down went the Federal infantry to a man, rear rank and front rank, and a forest of bayonet seemed growing there and waving in the weird twilight. Death was everywhere, but no one saw him. Only the gaping guns vomiting grape – only the infantry and cavalry heating the air with bullets were before the eyes of the fierce Missourians. One swift, short, hungry yell now and no more. The Federal cannoneers were devoted soldiers and deserved a better fate, the supports beyond fought well at first, but in the murderous pistol combat they were no match for the Missourians, and rushed away toward Westport, disorganized and broken.

As night fell, Curtis was forced to abandon his painstakingly fortified line along the Big Blue. The evening of October 22, Curtis held a council of war with his commanders. Curtis was now finally in contact with Pleasonton. Curtis' entire Federal line would then wheel 90 degrees to the right, attempting to arrange itself in an east-to-west line facing south. Curtis accordingly transferred his headquarters to the Gillis House in Kansas City. That evening Curtis wired Washington: "I am preparing to renew the attack and pursue it at daylight with all my available cavalry." However, by morning Curtis' army would still be moving into its new position.

On the Confederate side, Price also faced a difficult situation. Price's train of 600 heavily laden wagons and 3,000 cattle, east of the Big Blue River and plodding southwest towards New Santa Fe, was escorted only by Cabell's Brigade and a hodgepodge band of unarmed recruits under Colonel Charles Tyler. Price's main defense for his wagon train would be a frontal assault by the Shelby and Fagan Divisions, fixing Curtis' army in front of Westport long enough for Marmaduke's Division to shepherd Price's immense wagon train out of harm's way.

The October 23 action before Westport would again start as two separate battles: Brush Creek in the west, fought between Curtis' Army of the Border and Price's Shelby and Fagan Divisions; and Byram's Ford in the east, fought between Pleasonton's Missouri cavalry division and Price's Confederate rearguard, the Marmaduke Division. All three armies – Curtis' Army of the Border, Price's Army of Missouri, and Rosecrans' Army of the Department of Missouri – expected to attack at first light, October 23, yet none would be entirely in position by daybreak.

The battle of Brush Creek, morning of October 23

As day broke, most of Curtis' army was still en route from Kansas City to Westport, including Blair's 1,000 plus cavalry and Deitzler's 5,000 plus KSM. However, Blunt's Division of 2,600 cavalry was ready, having labored throughout the night to redeploy and fortify a new line on the north bank of the west-to-east-flowing Brush Creek.

October 23 dawned bitter and cold. Without waiting for Deitzler's and Blair's reinforcements, the outnumbered Blunt launched a spoiling attack south from Brush Creek shortly after 0700hrs. Blunt's main assault comprised the combined 1,500 cavalry of Colonel Jennison's 1st Brigade and Colonel Ford's 4th Brigade, led by the 2nd Colorado Cavalry in skirmish line.

To the south, Shelby's 3,000 cavalry and Fagan's 2,000 cavalry were supposed to launch their own screening attack at daybreak towards Westport. However, Shelby and Fagan were late getting into position, with

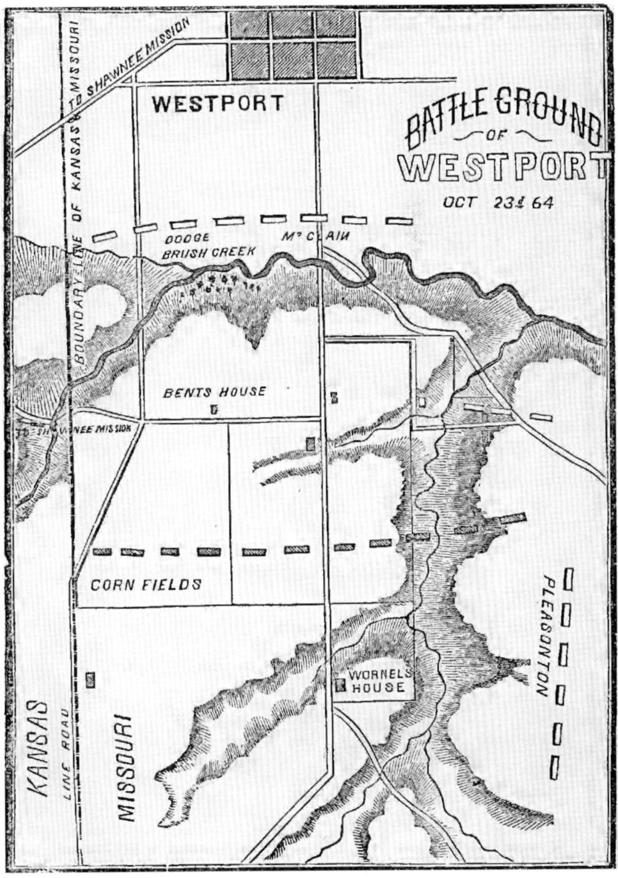

A map of the October 23, 1864 battle of Brush Creek. The Federal advance was an attempt to push the Confederates away from the Kansas border, barely a few miles to the west. Although heavily urbanized now, at the time the area was simple farmland and wooded, slightly rugged prairie. (Hinton, Richard J. (Richard Josiah), 1830–1901, public domain, via Wikimedia Commons)

LEFT
Famed Wild West mountain man Jeremiah "Liver-Eating" Johnson was a 40-year-old private in the 2nd Colorado Cavalry during the Westport campaign. Johnson likely was part of Blunt's skirmish line at the October 23, 1864 Federal advance at Brush Creek. (http://johnlivereatingjohnston.com/, public domain, via Wikimedia Commons)

RIGHT
Colonel Charles R. "Doc" Jennison of the 15th Kansas Cavalry commanded the 1st Brigade Cavalry, Army of the Border. The radical Jennison had a vigilante reputation and, after establishing the 7th Kansas Cavalry ("Jennison's Jayhawkers") in October 1861, Jennison would eventually raise and command the 15th Kansas Cavalry in late 1863. Jennison was frequently arrested for his jayhawking activities and was finally court-martialed and expelled in 1865. (kansasmemory.org, Kansas State Historical Society)

Shelby's Division departing camp only around 0800hrs and Fagan's taking another hour.

Battle opened just after 0800hrs when Blunt's and Shelby's advance units opened fire on each other north of the Wornall House, south of Westport. By 0930hrs, Shelby's and Fagan's troops had pushed the outnumbered Blunt division back to the north bank of Brush Creek, where the KSM was beginning to arrive. However, the Confederate attack began to stall as ammunition ran low, forcing Shelby to redeploy along a stone fence atop the bluff south of Brush Creek.

The battle of Byram's Ford, morning of October 23

At Byram's Ford, three miles to the east, Marmaduke's Division of 2,500 Confederate cavalry had crossed the Big Blue River at 0200hrs that morning, with the 1,000 troops of Freeman's Brigade deploying in a defensive position on the west bank of the ford. Behind them on Potato Hill, a high bluff to the west, they were supported by the 1,500 troops of Clark's Brigade. From here, the rearguard Marmaduke Division expected to hold off the Federals' Army of the Department of Missouri long enough for Price's wagon train to escape to the south.

Pleasonton's Missouri cavalry division had ended October 22 with McNeil's and Sanborn's 2nd and 3rd Brigades occupying Independence, and Brown's and Winslow's 1st and 4th Brigades having advanced west to within a few miles of the Big Blue River.

For October 23, Pleasonton expected to storm Marmaduke's Division at Byram's Ford with three brigades and thus cave in Price's entire Confederate rearguard on the Big Blue. The initial daybreak attack was to be made by Brigadier General Brown's Brigade, which was required to first pass through Winslow's Brigade in the dark. However, Brown was slowed by logistical complications, and was not ready to attack until 0815hrs. Almost simultaneously, an enraged Pleasonton galloped to the front and arrested Brown for failing to attack on

Battle of Byram's Ford, October 23

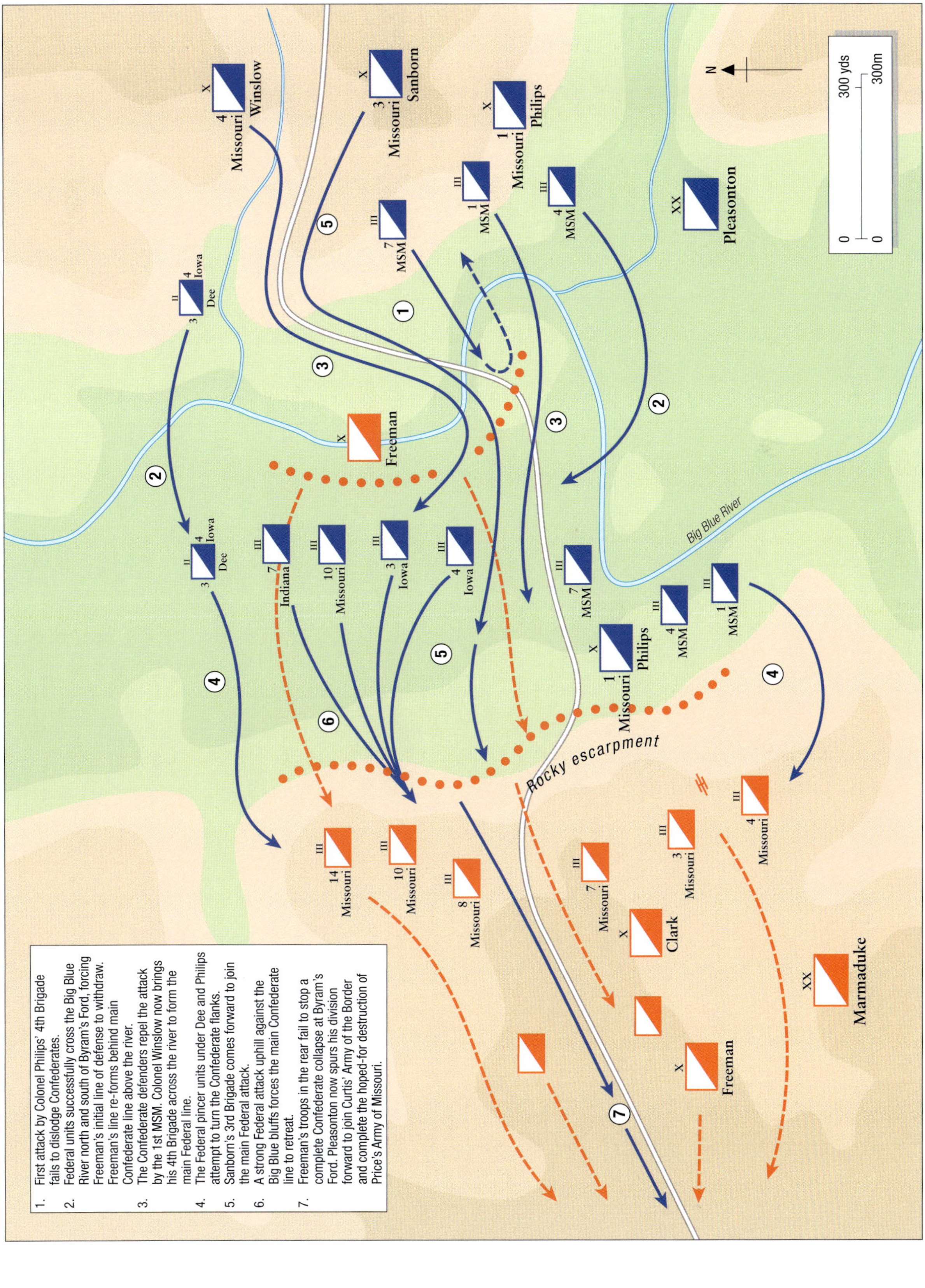

THE BATTLE OF WESTPORT, OCTOBER 20–23

Price's raid reaches its climax in the Kansas City–Westport region of northwest Missouri.

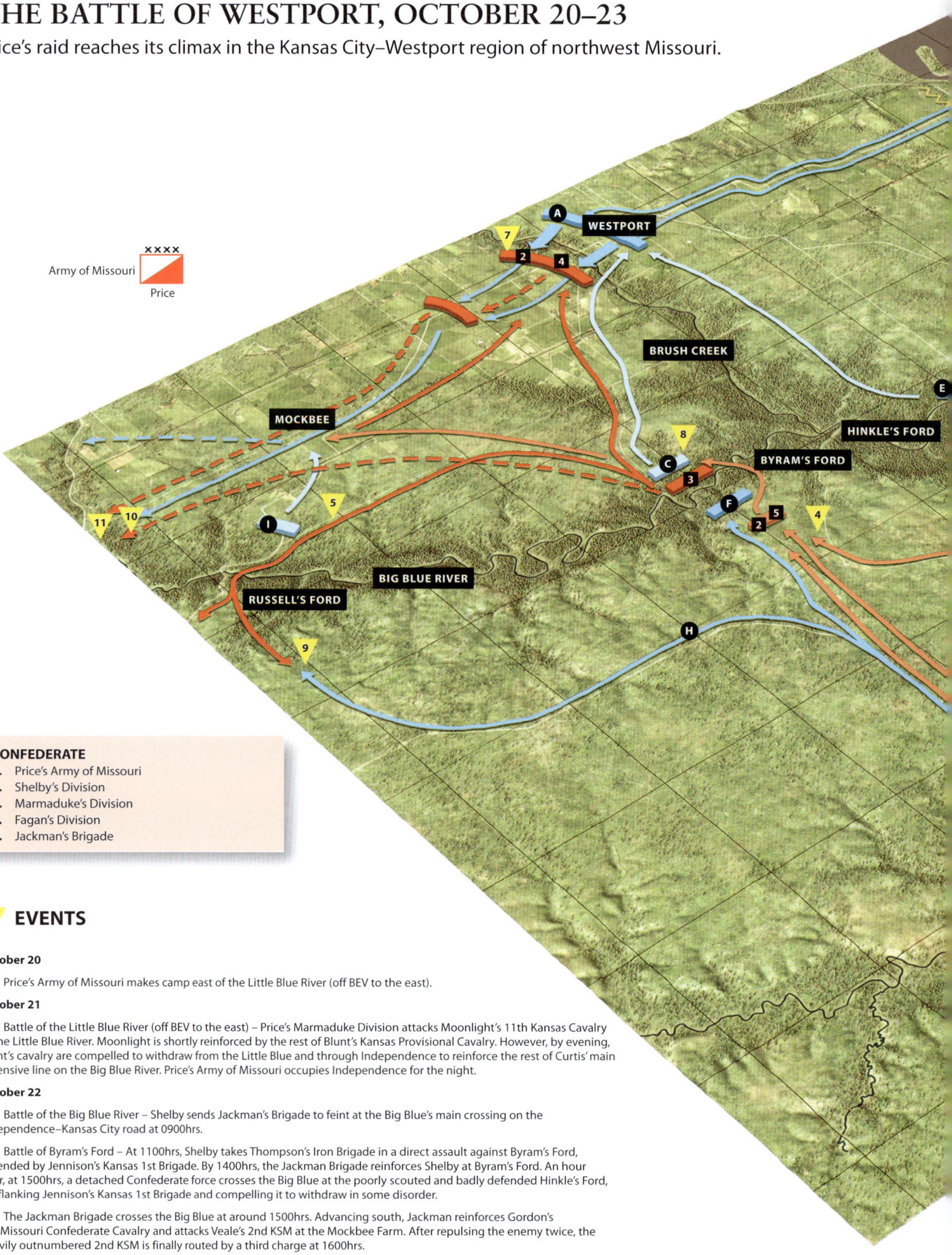

CONFEDERATE

1. Price's Army of Missouri
2. Shelby's Division
3. Marmaduke's Division
4. Fagan's Division
5. Jackman's Brigade

EVENTS

October 20

1. Price's Army of Missouri makes camp east of the Little Blue River (off BEV to the east).

October 21

2. Battle of the Little Blue River (off BEV to the east) – Price's Marmaduke Division attacks Moonlight's 11th Kansas Cavalry at the Little Blue River. Moonlight is shortly reinforced by the rest of Blunt's Kansas Provisional Cavalry. However, by evening, Blunt's cavalry are compelled to withdraw from the Little Blue and through Independence to reinforce the rest of Curtis' main defensive line on the Big Blue River. Price's Army of Missouri occupies Independence for the night.

October 22

3. Battle of the Big Blue River – Shelby sends Jackman's Brigade to feint at the Big Blue's main crossing on the Independence–Kansas City road at 0900hrs.

4. Battle of Byram's Ford – At 1100hrs, Shelby takes Thompson's Iron Brigade in a direct assault against Byram's Ford, defended by Jennison's Kansas 1st Brigade. By 1400hrs, the Jackman Brigade reinforces Shelby at Byram's Ford. An hour later, at 1500hrs, a detached Confederate force crosses the Big Blue at the poorly scouted and badly defended Hinkle's Ford, outflanking Jennison's Kansas 1st Brigade and compelling it to withdraw in some disorder.

5. The Jackman Brigade crosses the Big Blue at around 1500hrs. Advancing south, Jackman reinforces Gordon's 5th Missouri Confederate Cavalry and attacks Veale's 2nd KSM at the Mockbee Farm. After repulsing the enemy twice, the heavily outnumbered 2nd KSM is finally routed by a third charge at 1600hrs.

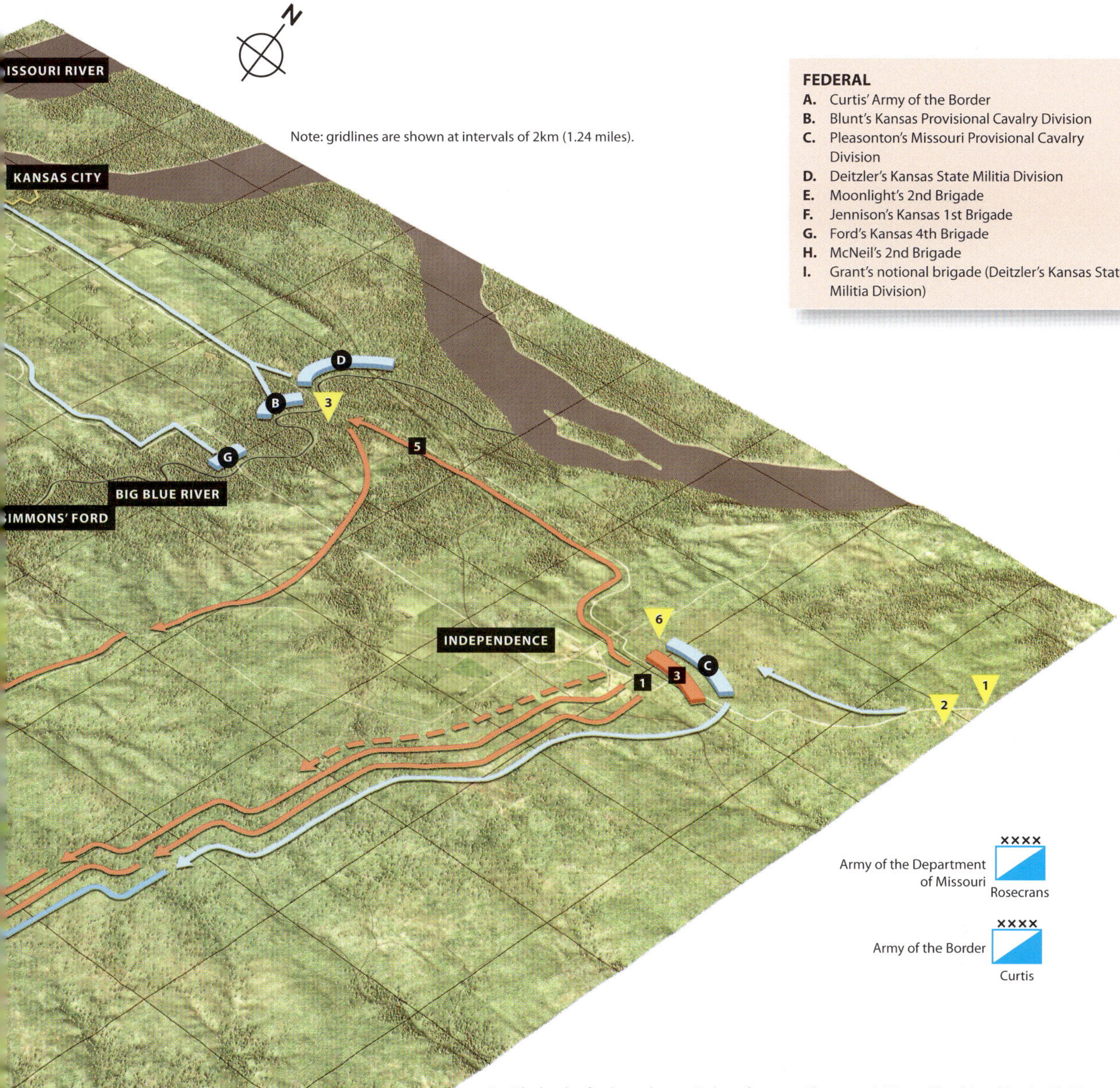

6. The battle of Independence – By late afternoon, Pleasonton's Missouri Provisional Cavalry Division has caught up with Price's rearguard at Independence. McNeil's 2nd Brigade and Sanborn's 3rd Brigade successfully drive the Cabell's Brigade and Slemons' Brigade out of town and towards Byram's Ford. They are pursued by Winslow's Missouri 4th Brigade until 2230hrs.

October 23

7. Battle of Brush Creek – At 0700hrs, Blunt orders Jennison's 1st Brigade and Ford's 4th Brigade south across Brush Creek in a spoiling attack against Confederate positions. Almost simultaneously, the Shelby and Fagan Divisions advance north into Blunt's attack. Outnumbered, Blunt is driven back across Brush Creek. By 1000hrs, significant Federal reinforcements have reached the creek. Curtis launches a major and coordinated assault across the creek but is driven back. Some time before 1200hrs, a local farmer, George Thoman, helps lead a Federal detachment through a hidden defile, enabling Curtis to deploy artillery into the Shelby Division's left flank. Shelby is forced to withdraw to the south.

8. Battle of Byram's Ford – Philips' Missouri 1st Brigade assaults Byram's Ford, but is driven back by the Marmaduke Division's defensive lines on the Big Blue's western bluffs. Winslow's 4th Brigade joins the attack. After several attempts, Philips' and Winslow's troops overcome the high Confederate defenses and force the Marmaduke Division to withdraw down the Harrisonville road.

9. McNeil's Missouri 2nd Brigade makes contact with Price's fleeing wagon train between Hickman Mills and New Santa Fe. McNeil fails to press the engagement, only exchanging skirmishing fire and long-range artillery fire with the escorting Cabell's Brigade, enabling Price's wagons to escape safely.

10. Curtis, Pleasonton, and Blunt meet at the Thoman farmhouse at 1430hrs to acknowledge the day's victory and plan their next moves.

11. Darkness falls, ending the Federals' immediate pursuit of Price. His Army of Missouri makes camp south of New Santa Fe on the middle fork of the Grand River (off BEV to the south).

Lieutenant Colonel Frederick W. Benteen, of the 10th Missouri Cavalry. Benteen is best remembered in history for the lackluster support he provided his doomed commander George Custer at the 1876 battle of the Little Big Horn. At Westport and Mine Creek, however, his courage and decisiveness were exemplary. (Public domain, via Wikimedia Commons)

time, promoting Colonel John Philips to brigade command and handing tactical control for the two-brigade crossing over to Winslow. Pleasonton would exercise overall command from the ford's eastern bluffs, where he was accompanied by Sanborn's Brigade in reserve, and the division artillery, which opened fire on the Confederate positions at 0900hrs.

Philips' Brigade of 1,500 dismounted troopers advanced south of the ford while being supported by Winslow's 1,200-strong 4th Brigade laying down skirmish fire to the north. After an initial repulse by Confederate fire, Captain Edward Dee's 3rd Battalion, 4th Iowa Cavalry snuck through a covered ravine 300 yards north of the ford, crossed to the west bank, and opened an enfilading fire into Freeman's 1,000 Confederate defenders. A second attack by Philips cleared Freeman's men from the west bank and successfully crossed the ford. Marmaduke ordered Freeman's reeling Confederates to re-form behind Clark's 1,500 men defending the Potato Hill heights.

Philips' troops were now across the ford but Winslow's were not. Winslow ordered Philips' men to make an immediate frontal charge up the heights into Clark's defensive line atop the ridge to cover Winslow's crossing. Funneled by the unfavorable terrain, Philips' cavalry were repulsed twice, but Winslow's Brigade was also across the river.

By 1100hrs, Winslow was able to make a coordinated attack up the heights with both his and Philips' Brigades, a combined 2,800 dismounted Federal troopers. They assaulted into the teeth of Clark's 1,500 men, but were driven off by intense fire just short of the rocky outcrop forming the Confederate skirmish line partway along the ridge.

Winslow ordered a second attack, which broke the Confederate skirmish line on the rocky escarpment. Marmaduke was forced to withdraw his artillery batteries and reposition them to the rear with Freeman's Brigade, a sight that further encouraged the Federal troopers. Winslow was shot and wounded, which slightly stalled his brigade's attack, until Lieutenant Colonel Frederick Benteen of the 10th Missouri rallied Winslow's troops and continued the uphill assault.

The surging Federals swarmed around Clark's faltering men. Both the 10th Missouri and 4th Iowa were attacking upwards in a frontal assault, but the Confederates were finally unhinged by a battalion of 4th Iowans assaulting from the northern flank, and Philips' Brigade working its way up a wooden ravine to the south. Marmaduke briefly tried to make a final stand with Freeman's men, but the sight of fresh Federal troops and guns pouring towards him inspired Marmaduke to withdraw.

It was now 1200hrs. Pleasonton ordered Sanborn's Brigade, hitherto in reserve on the east banks of the Big Blue, to pursue the Confederates. The second battle of Byram's Ford had been an unusually fierce action, with about 400 casualties on each side. However, the way was now open for Rosecrans' Army of the Department of Missouri to link up with the Kansans of Curtis' Army of the Border.

The battle of Brush Creek, midday on October 23

Back at Brush Creek, three miles to the west, Curtis had been waging his own fight to dislodge Price's stubborn Confederates. The large mass of

Kansas City's high-end Country Club Plaza and its accompanying Brush Creek seen in a modern-day photograph. On October 23, 1864, the Federals attacked from the north of the creek (attacking right to left in the photograph), assembling where the Plaza's famous Christmas lights decorate the district today. Very little remains to memorialize the battle now. (User:Charvex, public domain, via Wikimedia Commons)

Kansas militiamen and guns had slowly trickled in throughout the morning, eventually assembling into their own separate brigade alongside Blunt's. As Curtis, Blunt, and Deitzler all planned the main attack, the Federals kept the pressure on with heavy cannon fire from 30 guns above Brush Creek and intense skirmishing along the wooded front line by the 2nd Colorado Cavalry and the 12th KSM.

Around 1100hrs, Curtis felt prepared to launch his coordinated attack, which he would lead in person. However, Blair's 3rd Brigade would advance prematurely to counter a perceived Confederate flank attempt. With Blunt on the left and Deitzler on the right, Curtis' now partly disjointed attack staggered forward across Brush Creek, but it stalled in the face of Shelby's Confederate defensive line on the stone fence atop Brush Creek's southern heights. Indeed Curtis was unable to bring his artillery forward through the thick timber to support the advance, while the guns were themselves masked by the terrain. Curtis' army fell back across the northern banks of Brush Creek, with some uncoordinated Federals remaining on the south bank continuing to skirmish with Shelby's Confederates.

A local German farmer, 75-year-old George Thoman, suddenly approached Curtis' sentries. Thoman, it seems, was incensed at Confederate soldiers looting his home the previous night. In a timeless scene recalling Thermopylae, the vengeful Thoman offered to reveal a hidden path wide enough for artillery that would flank the Confederate lines entirely. Curtis dispatched Captain Dodge's 9th Wisconsin Battery and two additional guns from Colonel Blair's brigade artillery; with Thoman personally leading the way, this impromptu Federal force began working through Thoman's wooded defile towards Brush Creek.

Shelby simply had too few men to adequately guard every approach. Further, particularly aggressive Federal skirmishing by Ford's brigade that morning near Wornall Lane may have convinced him that the main Federal assault was to come here, and not through Thoman's path half a mile to the southwest, defended by a thin skirmish line of the Jackman Brigade.

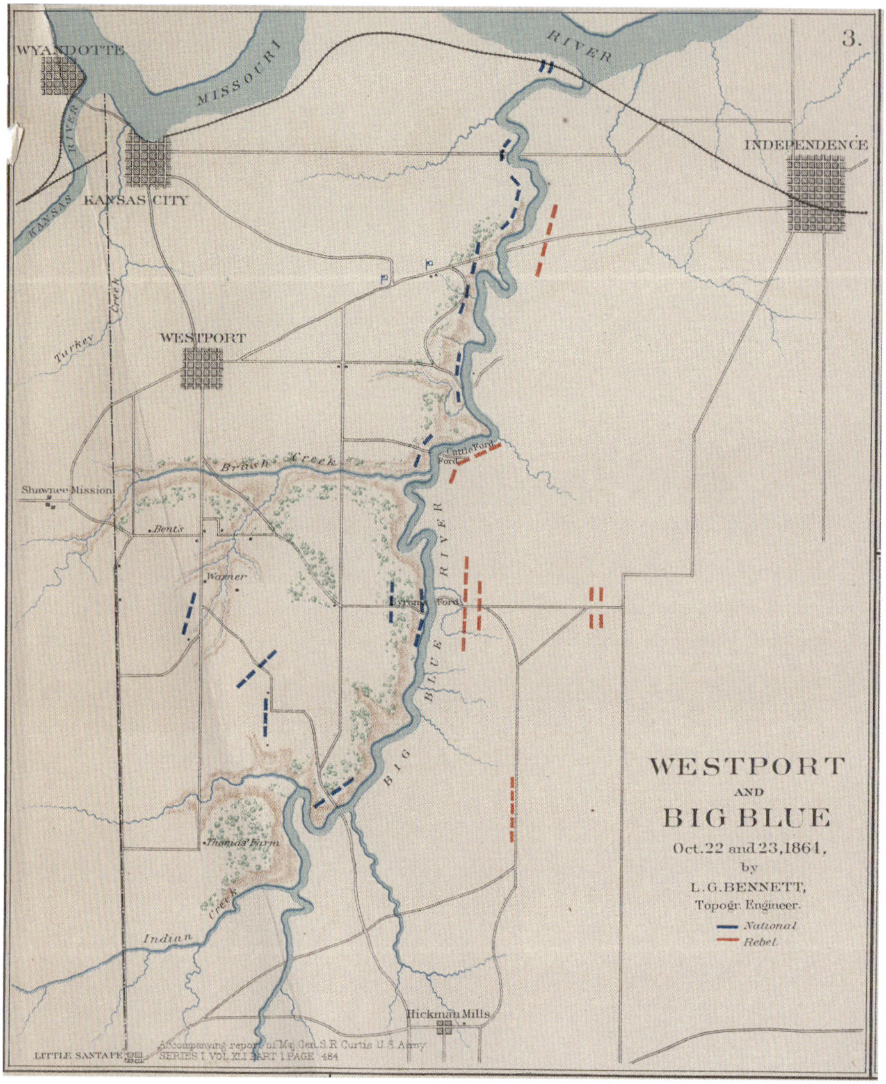

An official map of the battle of Westport, produced in Curtis' after-action report. Westport was the largest land battle ever west of the Mississippi River, and its subsequent obscurity in Civil War histories is one of the Kansas–Missouri region's great cultural losses. (kansasmemory.org, Kansas State Historical Society)

Colonel Charles W. Blair of the 14th Kansas Cavalry commanded Blunt's 3rd Brigade, which consisted almost entirely of mounted Kansas State Militia. Blair would return to his law practice after the war, eventually dying in California in 1899. (Cberk6, CC BY-SA 4.0 https://creativecommons.org/licenses/by-sa/4.0, via Wikimedia Commons)

It was here, at the Bent House, that Blair's 3rd Brigade of Federals, accompanied by Curtis' personal escort, erupted out of Thoman's farm path. Jackman's outnumbered skirmishers opened a heavy fire from a cornfield, but were soon routed by the Blair attack. Curtis moved Dodge's artillery up to the Bent House, enabling him to fire into the Thompson Brigade, comprising Shelby's left flank. Shelby was now forced to withdraw to a second defensive line half a mile to the southeast. Under Blunt, the Jennison and Ford Brigades were able to seize the southern heights above Brush Creek.

Curtis and Blunt consolidated their forces on the heights and brought up 30 artillery pieces, both regular and militia, and began to pound the eight guns remaining to Price. Curtis ordered the Federal advance renewed. During the attack, McLain's Colorado Battery unlimbered along Wornall Lane and began hammering Confederate positions.

Battle of Brush Creek, October 23

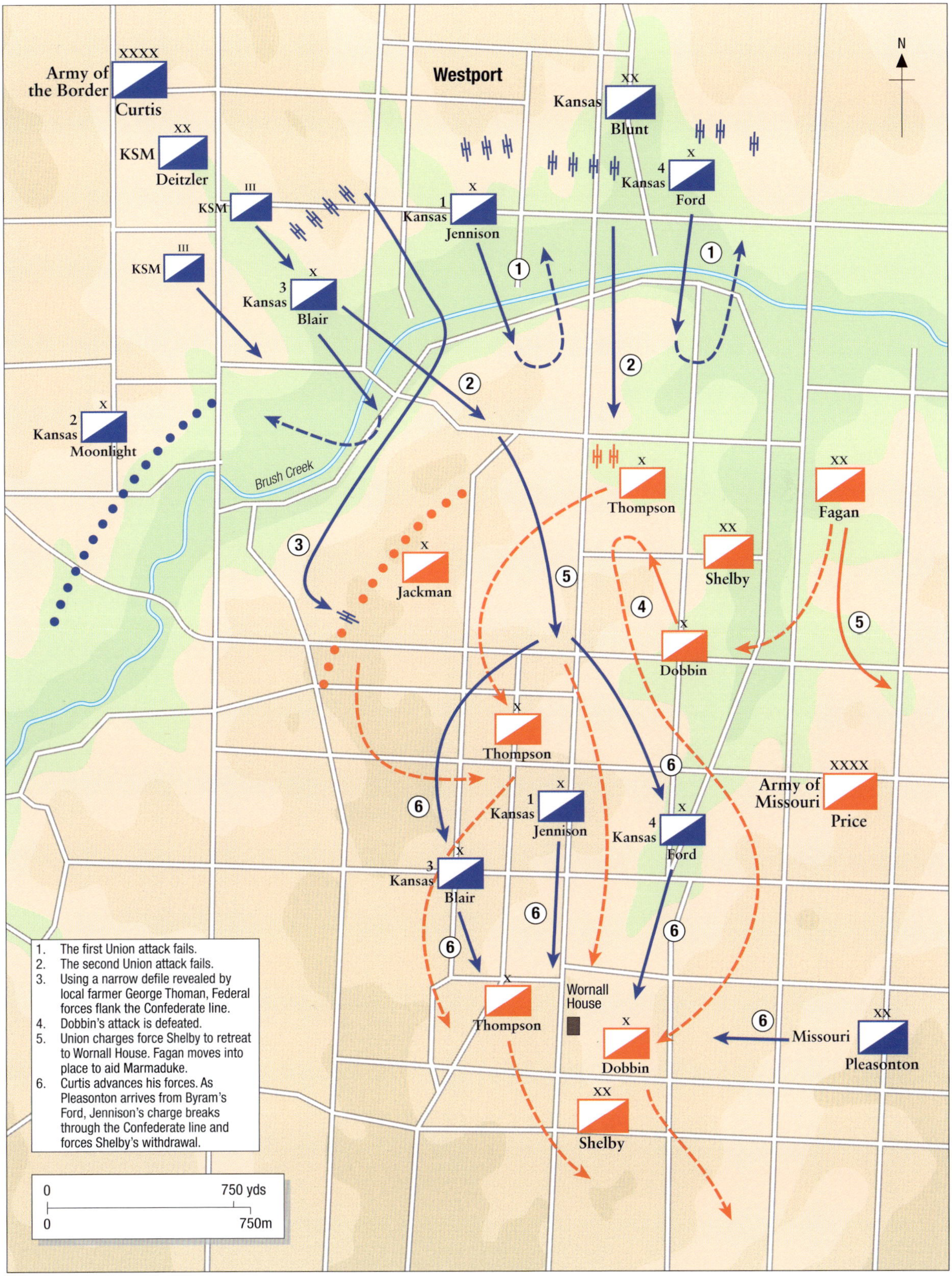

In response, Colonel James McGhee, commanding Confederate Arkansas Cavalry from Price's Fagan Division, ordered a desperate charge against the Colorado Battery, exposed in front of the Federal lines. Colonel Jennison ordered a counterattack by his Company E Jayhawkers of the 15th Kansas Cavalry. A furious cavalry battle ensued which routed the Confederates, wounding McGhee, killing 25, and taking over 100 prisoners.

Shelby fell back to a last desperate stand along a stone fence at the Wornall House, commanding his own two Confederate brigades and Dobbin's Brigade from Fagan's Division.

The time was now 1200hrs and events began to happen rapidly. It was at this time that Pleasonton, three miles to the east at Byram's Ford, began his hell-for-leather pursuit to crush Marmaduke's fleeing men and link up with Curtis. Meanwhile, Price, who had been with Shelby all morning, received word the wagon train was in danger; Price headed southeast with Jackman's troops to protect the wagon train.

Curtis now had Shelby where he wanted him and ordered Jennison's 1,000 Jayhawker cavalry to break Shelby's lines at the Wornall House on Wornall Lane. Simultaneously, Pleasonton defeated Fagan's reeling troops and brushed aside Jackman's reinforcements. Sanborn's Brigade, in Pleasonton's vanguard, which occupied Hinkle's Grove 500 yards to the east of the Wornall House, opened an enfilading fire into Shelby's flank. Thompson's elite Iron Brigade suddenly collapsed in a stampeding route to the south. The Confederate front lines were shattered.

Incredibly, Shelby managed to partly rally his men and set up another defensive line one mile to the south, slowing the Federal breakthrough by Curtis enough to buy some time. Farther to the south, Pleasonton's 2nd Brigade, under McNeil, had left Independence early that morning for Hickman Mills to cut off a Price escape, but arrived late. McNeil skirmished half-heartedly with Price's wagon train escort, sighting the train three times

A modern-day view of Kansas City's Wornall House, which Curtis used as his headquarters and in which both Federals and Confederates tended their wounded as a makeshift hospital. The area around the Wornall House was one of the final battlefields of the battle of Westport on October 23. (User:Iknowthegoods, CC BY-SA 3.0 https://creativecommons.org/licenses/by-sa/3.0, via Wikimedia Commons)

A modern-day view of Kansas City's Loose Park, featuring several cannon. The Union's superiority in artillery was a major factor in the battle of Westport. The battle itself was sprawling and Loose Park is one of the few areas of modern-day Kansas City that still memorializes the battle. (Americasroof, CC BY-SA 3.0 https://creativecommons.org/licenses/by-sa/3.0, via Wikimedia Commons)

that afternoon, but never pursuing vigorously. In addition, Price's men set fire to the prairie grass to obscure their flight. By 1300hrs the train had largely escaped immediate danger. At 1430hrs the Federal commanders conferred at Thoman Farm to celebrate the great victory. However, even then, the potentially devastating pursuit was being botched by Federal subordinates. Price's badly defeated Army of Missouri retreated south with its bloated wagon train relatively intact – for now.

Although the Confederates' Army of Missouri was in clear retreat, Curtis deemed "a vigorous pursuit" necessary to keep Price from mauling the numerous scattered Federal outposts between Kansas City and the Arkansas River. However, as Westport historian Howard Monett put so well, "The Union forces had become as thoroughly disorganized in victory as the Confederate forces had in defeat."

Around 1700hrs, October 23, Curtis rescinded martial law in Kansas, allowed Kansas militiamen north of Aubry to go home, and agreed with Rosecrans, now in Independence, that the pursuit force would consist of Blunt's Provisional Cavalry Division (Kansas) and Pleasonton's Provisional Cavalry Division (Missouri). This combined force of Federals bivouacked at New Santa Fe the night of October 23/24. The tail of Price's bloated wagon train was just eight miles to the south.

Official casualty reports for October 21–23 claim a combined total of 240 killed, 868 wounded, and 437 captured between the two sides, for an official combined casualty figure of 1,545. However, the actual combined figure may have been closer to 3,500.

THE FEDERAL PURSUIT, OCTOBER 24–28

Curtis, Blunt, and Pleasonton now awkwardly combined the two Federal departments' forces to pursue Price. As senior officer present, Curtis took command of the combined Kansas–Missouri force, and resumed the pursuit the following morning. However, Price had refused to abandon his wagon train and was only slowly making his way south, to the consternation of his experienced cavalrymen, who knew they could easily make 50 miles a day rather than the 28 miles they would average. On October 24, Price's reeling army, whose discipline verged on collapse, crossed the state line into Linn

County, Kansas, the longtime epicenter of Jayhawker raids into Missouri. Price's largely Missouri troops were already in a foul mood. They immediately began mass plundering Linn County farms and murdered a number of Kansas civilians. Late that evening, thunderstorms began to fall on farmlands already battered and burned by drought and years of guerrilla raids. Pursuing Federal troops, many of them Linn County natives, became increasingly outraged at the civilian destruction they observed in the Confederates' wake. The Federal force finally made camp at Trading Post, Kansas, six miles north of the Marais des Cygnes River, at 0230hrs, October 25.

A late-night war council between Curtis, Blunt, and Pleasonton saw Blunt urge a highly risky but potentially devastating flanking maneuver: a 15-mile forced march completely around Price in the night. However, the more conservative Curtis overruled Blunt, believing a frontal assault to be less operationally risky. Pleasonton, exhausted and increasingly disenchanted with his Missouri cavalry's continued involvement, ultimately backed Curtis. His strategy rejected, Blunt appears to have retreated into an unproductive sulk.

The battle of Marais des Cygnes, morning of October 25

Early October 25 saw Price's Army of Missouri with Shelby's Division in the vanguard, Fagan's Division covering the western flank, and Marmaduke's Division in the rearguard. Around midnight, Price headed down the Fort Scott road, intent on capturing southeast Kansas' Fort Scott for supplies.

Claiming illness, Pleasonton delegated field command to Sanborn, whose 3rd Brigade had already skirmished with Price's rearguard at 0200hrs, even bombarding the Confederates with cannon. Around 0500hrs, the 2nd Colorado and 2nd Arkansas Cavalry of Sanborn's 3rd Brigade drove south and attacked the rearguard Marmaduke Division skirmish line, successfully driving the Confederates off a pair of round 140ft hills north of the Marais des Cygnes River called the Mounds. A mile to the south, the 8th Provisional EMM drove another Confederate skirmish line back across the Marais des Cygnes.

With Marmaduke entirely across the Marais des Cygnes, Sanborn captured 100 prisoners, two cannons, and some wagons north of the river. The 2nd Arkansas Cavalry now led a Federal crossing to the southern bank.

Marmaduke's own rearguard, the Clark Brigade, promptly assembled in line to block the Federal advance. Upon crossing the river, Sanborn assembled his own line, when he was suddenly gripped by indecision. Sanborn delegated command to Colonel John Phelps of the 2nd Arkansas Cavalry, then departed to personally seek clarification from superiors. Phelps now attacked Clark in defiance of his standing orders from Sanborn, and was ultimately repulsed within sight of Curtis, Pleasonton, and Sanborn riding back to the front.

Pleasonton reassumed divisional command from Sanborn at 0900hrs and shortly had 3,500 troops across the Marais des Cygnes facing Clark's 1,200 defenders. With Phelps' 2nd Arkansas threatening to flank him, Clark admitted defeat and withdrew at 1000hrs.

The battle of Mine Creek, midday on October 25

Price and the Shelby Division remained some miles ahead; indeed Price still expected to capture Fort Scott and remained largely ignorant of the disaster approaching from his rear.

Price's route took his army over Mine Creek, a Kansas tributary of the Osage River. Mine Creek was not particularly wide, swift, or deep, but its

Battle of Mine Creek, October 25

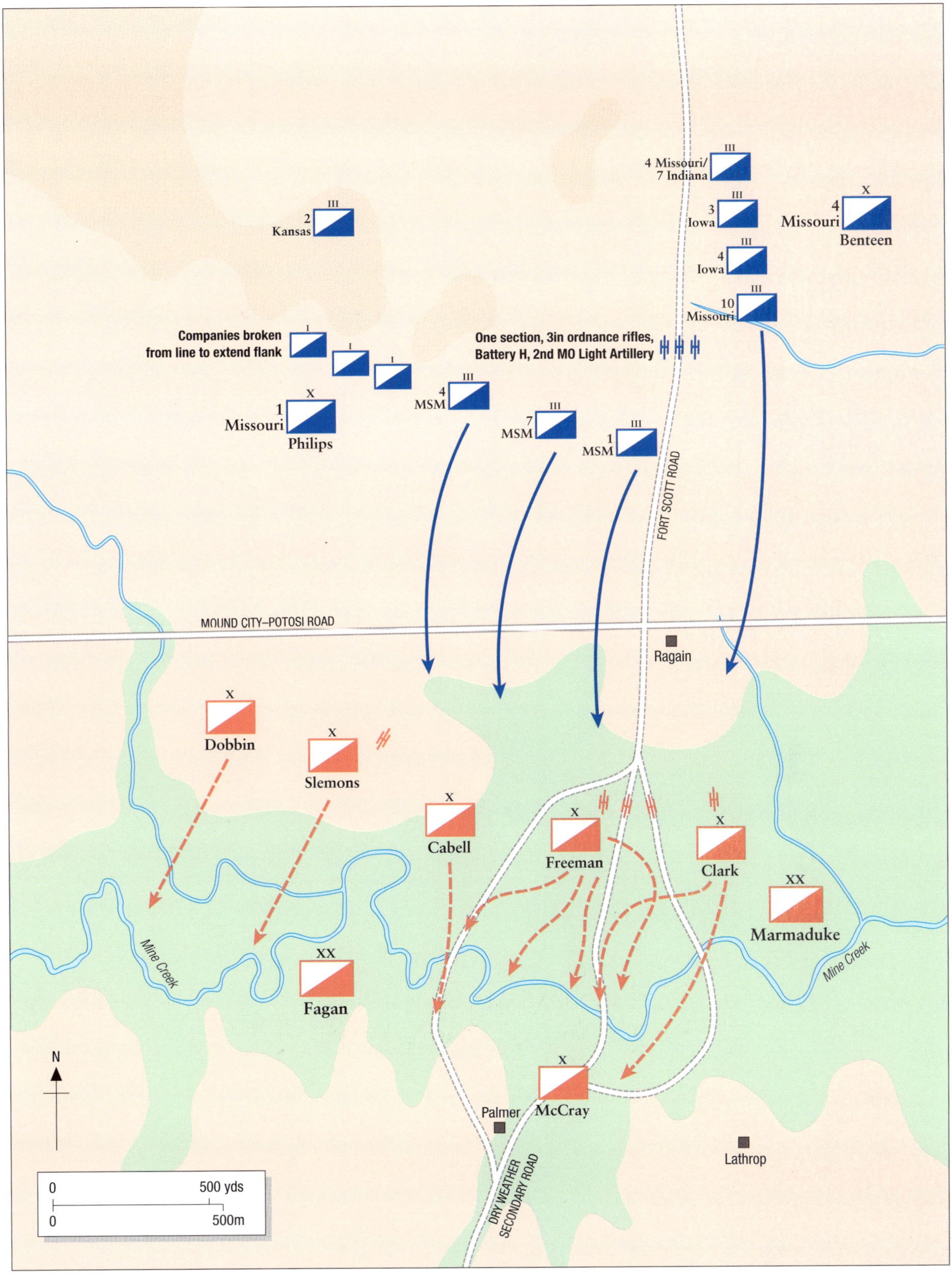

BATTLE OF MINE CREEK, 1100HRS, OCTOBER 25 (PP.84–85)

Mine Creek's only passable ford required wagons to enter the creek from its northern banks, turn left and travel 25 yards over the rock-bottomed creek bed itself, then turn right and climb up the steep, muddy southern bank. The passage of hundreds of wagons and throusands of livestock shortly churned the ford's banks into a quagmire. By 1100hrs, about a dozen Confederate wagons and 6,300 troops remained stranded on the north side of Mine Creek. At this moment, nearly 3,000 mounted Federal cavalry appeared to the north of the creek. With no easy way to retreat, the Confederates drew up defensive lines.

Union Colonel John Philips recalled, "The sun was just coming above the fog of the river bottom and spreading its golden light over the plain. It gleamed on thousands of guns and sabers being drawn for carnage." Within minutes, the mounted Federals had closed to 500 yards of the Confederate line and began a galloping charge through heavy infantry and artillery fire.

However, saddled with single-shot muzzle-loaders, the Confederates could only get off three or four rounds before the Federal charge clammed into them **(1)**. In the furious melee that ensued, the Confederates' long rifles **(2)** were hopelessly outmatched by the Federals' sabers, pistols, and rapid-firing carbines; the 4th Iowa's Major Abial Pierce cut down eight Confederates with his saber alone. Despite being outnumbered more than 2:1, the Federal cavalry completely shattered the demoralized veterans of nearly two whole Confederate divisions in barely half an hour.

Samuel J. Reader, a Kansas militia prisoner of the Confederates, portrays the Federal attack on Price's army at Mine Creek. Reader and his fellow Kansas prisoners had to endure deprivation at the hands of the Confederates who were nearly starving and freezing themselves. Reader and the surviving Kansas prisoners were eventually freed shortly after Mine Creek. (Kansas Historical Society, public domain, via Wikimedia Commons)

12–15ft-high banks on both sides were steep and muddy. The Confederate wagon train began crossing, but by 1100hrs the muddy ford had been churned into a quagmire. Many wagons and most of the Fagan and Marmaduke Divisions remained on the northern side of Mine Creek when Federal cavalry was spotted approaching 500 yards away across the flat and open prairie. Fagan, Marmaduke, and Clark, commanding the rearguard, felt no choice but to stand and fight. About 6,300 Confederate cavalrymen remained north of the creek; the Confederate lines extended about 800 yards across and included eight cannon.

At 1100hrs, two Federal cavalry brigades burst over the low ridge north of Mine Creek; these were Pleasonton's 1st and 4th Brigades, now commanded by Colonel John Philips and Lieutenant Colonel Frederick Benteen respectively. Attached to each Federal brigade was a six-gun horse artillery battery of 3in rifled cannon. The combined Federal force numbered 2,700 cavalry and 12 guns. Over the next 30 minutes they would engage over 7,000 Confederates.

The battle of Mine Creek began at 1100hrs when Benteen surprisingly ordered a mounted mass cavalry charge, a maneuver already considered virtually suicidal by 1864. Philips' Brigade shortly followed; the image of nearly 3,000 mounted Federal cavalry charging across the open Kansas prairie at full gallop must have been among the most spectacular sights of the entire Civil War.

When Major William Lusk's 10th Missouri, leading Benteen's charge on the Federal right, began to stall under severe Confederate canister fire, Major Abial Pierce's 4th Iowa galloped around them and reignited the attack. Benteen's and Philips' mounted Federal charge slammed into the exhausted and poorly armed Confederates and led to one of the most one-sided battles of the war, routing most of the Marmaduke and Fagan Divisions on the north bank of Mine Creek in just half an hour. By 1130hrs, the bulk of the close-quarters violence had ended. The dramatic charge had blown the Federals' horses, ensuring no pursuit in strength was possible. What action remained settled down into long-range skirmishing.

The Federals had lost a shockingly low eight killed and 72 wounded. In contrast the Confederates had suffered a staggering 1,280 casualties, including over 300 killed and 237 wounded. The terrific killed-to-wounded ratio – five

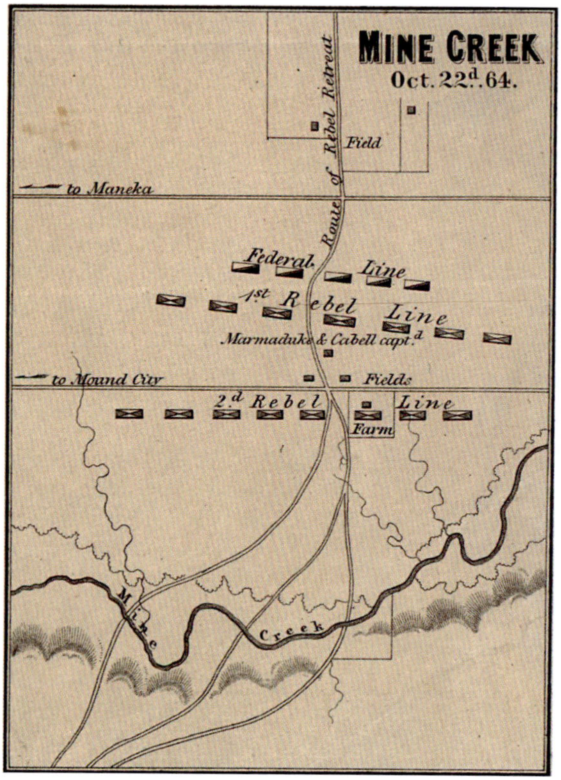

An official Federal map of the battle of Mine Creek, produced for a report after the battle. Mine Creek was unusual in many aspects and represents the long-delayed climactic collapse of Price's army two days after its clear defeat at Westport. (Library of Congress, public domain, via Wikimedia Commons)

times higher than usual – darkly suggests that most Confederate dead had been massacred by vengeful Federals after they had surrendered. Finally, all eight Confederate guns and nearly 600 Confederate troops had been captured, including one division commander and two brigade commanders: Major General John Marmaduke, Brigadier General William Cabell, and Colonel William Slemons.

Incredibly, three additional Federal brigades – Sanborn's, McNeil's, and Blunt's – had been just miles away along the Marais des Cygnes and none had ridden to the sound of the guns. It hardly mattered; Benteen's and Philips' two brigades had simply mauled a large proportion of Price's disintegrating army. Only Price, much of the wagon train, and the Shelby Division – all already over Mine Creek – survived in any capacity.

Despite lasting just 30 minutes, the October 25, 1864 battle of Mine Creek was the second-largest cavalry battle of the American Civil War; it was by far the war's most successful mounted cavalry charge – likely the largest mounted cavalry charge in American history – and at nearly 10,000 combatants remains the largest single battle ever fought in the state of Kansas.

The battle of Marmiton River, evening of October 25

Late in the day, what remained of Price's column again crossed the state line, but the Confederate wagon train stalled once more while fording the Marmiton River in Vernon County, Missouri.

Once again the Confederates were forced to make an impromptu stand on the near bank of a river to protect their train. Forming into line were Thompson's Iron Brigade, some Mine Creek survivors of the Fagan and Marmaduke Divisions, Colonel Tyler's Brigade, who were mostly unarmed recruits, and the Jackman Brigade, whom Shelby held in reserve.

The Confederate defensive line shortly sighted oncoming Federal cavalry of McNeil's 2nd Brigade and Benteen's 4th Brigade. Shelby ordered a charge by some of Tyler's men which the Federals easily repulsed. The Federals now brought up cannon. Shelby gamely attempted several feints at the Federals, but these too failed. After realizing their guns would be masked by their own charge, the Federals redeployed their artillery. However, by the time the Federals commenced their charge, they realized their horses were too tired to gallop.

Exhausted and demoralized, some Confederates began retreating on their own. As night began to fall, Shelby unleashed the reserve Jackman Brigade for a charge which drove back the 4th Iowa Cavalry. With both sides exhausted, the surviving Confederates were able to withdraw under cover of night.

Federal casualties are unknown, but were light. Confederate casualties were about 25 dead and 50 wounded. Price finally ordered much of the remaining wagon train burned. Price's total losses since daybreak came to over 300 killed, over 250 wounded, and nearly 700 captured, plus eight of 11 cannons lost and most of the expedition's wagon train destroyed. October 25 had been a calamitous day for the Confederates.

The battle of Albany, October 26

We must now briefly leave the main drama between Price and his Federal pursuers and return to northwest Missouri. By now Missouri authorities had redoubled their efforts to defeat Quantrill's Raiders and kill their current leader Bloody Bill Anderson once and for all. The experienced Colonel S.P. Cox was assigned to take Anderson out and was provided with veteran members of the 33rd EMM to help him.

After Anderson's location was reported by a local woman, Colonel Cox set up a guerrilla-style ambush at Albany in Clay County, Missouri. Cox turned the tables on the bushwhackers by tricking them into charging a seemingly weak Unionist position at Albany on October 26. In fact, Cox had 130 armed troops with him. Anderson and six other bushwhackers were shot dead to zero militia members killed. Anderson's body was shortly paraded through the streets. Among the items found on Anderson's body were two October 11 orders from Price. Cox's successful ambush and killing of Anderson immediately made him a Missouri state hero.

The body of Bloody Bill Anderson, photographed hours after his death in Albany, Missouri. Anderson's body was paraded through the streets and partially mutilated after his killing, just as Anderson had done to his own victims. Two orders from Price were found on Anderson's body. (Robert B. Kice, public domain, via Wikimedia Commons)

The battle of Newtonia, October 28

After the disastrous October 25 battles, Price's Army of Missouri now largely consisted of what was left of the Shelby Division. Although Federal forces were dwindling as many units were released to go home, Curtis continued his pursuit, closing an eight-hour gap to less than three hours by October 26. Price's army also continued to dwindle thanks to deserters and often starving or wounded stragglers; many of these appear to have been murdered upon discovery by Federal pursuers. By October 28, Price's crumbling army had taken a small Federal outpost in Newtonia in southwest Missouri, killing its commander Lieutenant Robert Christian possibly after he surrendered.

However, about 1,000 cavalry under Blunt's 1st and 4th Brigades quickly arrived, still in pursuit. Price could only muster about 2,500 tired troops under Shelby as a rearguard; Shelby's battered division was almost all that was left of Price's army anyway. Nevertheless, the Confederates attacked the outnumbered Blunt force and began to drive it back, before Curtis and Sanborn arrived with perhaps another 1,000 cavalry from Fort Scott that evening. The battle continued until about 2100hrs, when both sides withdrew exhausted but claiming victory. Estimates vary widely, but casualties were about equal at around 100 each.

Newtonia proved the campaign's last battle of any significance. The following day, October 29, two Federal brigades were withdrawn from the Price pursuit per Grant's orders; no more Federal strength was to be wasted west of the Mississippi. Curtis continued pursuing Price's deteriorating army south before abandoning the chase at the Arkansas River on November 8. To avoid Fort Smith, Price marched west and then south through the Indian Territory and Texas before turning east and re-entering Arkansas on December 2, effectively signaling the end of the disastrous Price Raid.

Never modest, Price later reported that he "had marched 1,434 miles, fought 43 battles and skirmishes, captured and paroled over 3,000 Federal officers and men, captured 18 pieces of artillery … and destroyed Missouri property … over $10 million in value." In reality, almost Price's entire Army of Missouri had been destroyed and none of its objectives had been accomplished.

Ironically, it was Price who pacified Missouri for the Union by recruiting most of the worst pro-Confederate guerrillas; those that survived the campaign simply accompanied Price in his withdrawal from the state. Of the three most notorious Missouri bushwhacker chieftains, George Todd had been shot and killed at Westport on October 22 and Bloody Bill Anderson had been ambushed and killed at nearby Albany on October 26, leaving only William Quantrill on the run.

By early 1865, Quantrill and his men had slipped into Kentucky. Quantrill's end proved strikingly similar to Anderson's. On May 10, Quantrill would be ambushed, shot, and captured at Taylorsville, Kentucky. Quantrill would linger in agony in a Louisville military prison before dying on June 6, 1865.

The modern Kansas City skyline lies about four miles north of Blunt's front line at Brush Creek the morning of October 23, 1864. Kansas City itself lies 120 miles north of Arkansas, making Westport the deepest any Confederate army penetrated into the Union during the American Civil War. (Dean Hochman, CC BY 2.0 https://creativecommons.org/licenses/by/2.0, via Wikimedia Commons)

AFTERMATH

Westport was the largest battle ever fought west of the Mississippi River, and virtually ended the Civil War in the West. It remains the largest battle ever fought in the American Midwest. Westport also provided a climactic end to the ten years of politically charged chaos and intimate, unrestrained violence that had gripped Kansas and Missouri since 1855.

According to Albert Castel in *General Sterling Price and the Civil War in the West*:

> [The] expedition failed to seize St. Louis or occupy Jefferson City and install a Confederate government, failed to bring about a mass uprising of Southern sympathizers, failed to influence state elections except probably to increase the Republican vote, and failed to do any damage to the Union military installations in Kansas. In fact Price failed to achieve a single one of his objectives other than to obtain recruits, and he did that only in the imperfect fashion described.

The twin Federal victories in Missouri and Kansas – Westport and Mine Creek – were overshadowed by Grant's and Sherman's successes in Virginia

The Price Raid of late 1864 essentially ended the Civil War in Missouri, one of the most war-torn states of the Union. To Major Samuel Byers, "Missouri was neither North or South, she was simply hell, for her people were cutting one another's throat, and neighboring farmers killed each other and burned each other's home." (Kansas Historical Society, public domain, via Wikimedia Commons)

and Georgia. However, a major Confederate triumph at St. Louis, Jefferson City, Westport, or Kansas may very well have put Lincoln's re-election in peril.

Lincoln won re-election on November 8, 1864, winning 22 states (including Kansas and Missouri) and losing three, while winning the electoral vote 212 to 21. Lincoln's decisive re-election ensured the Union would fight the war to a victorious finish. In contrast, the incumbent Kansas Governor Thomas Carney would lose his bid for re-election to his Radical Republican opponent Samuel J. Crawford.

Missouri would see the third most combat actions of the Civil War, trailing only Virginia and Tennessee in total engagements. By war's end in 1865, nearly 110,000 Missourians had served with the Union Army while over 40,000 had served with the Confederate Army. These numbers do not include large numbers of local and state militia, or the irregular bushwhacker guerrillas.

Kansas City, a modest town in 1860, boomed from the 1870s cattle industry and would grow to rival St. Louis in size and importance, eventually anchoring western Missouri and becoming the state of Kansas' largest metropolitan area. Missouri's cultural connection to the South would slowly fade over the next 100 years, and by the late 20th century, Missouri would generally become identified with the Midwest, although Southern connections remain strong south of the Missouri River.

In 1861, Kansas had about 30,000 men between the ages of 18 and 45. By war's end, over 20,000 would have volunteered to fight for the Union in Kansas regiments. Of these, over 8,500 would be killed, giving Kansas the highest proportion of both volunteers and fatalities of any state in the Union. Kansas also gave a higher share of its 1864 vote to Lincoln than any other Northern state. Overall, the Civil War was good to Kansas, despite the Lawrence and Baxter Springs disasters. The state's farm acreage, farm value, and total land value all more than doubled between 1861 and 1865.

Kansas continued its westward settlement and would not suffer its last Plains Indian raid until 1878, 13 years after the Confederacy's downfall. Kansas remained politically radical and progressive, becoming the first US state to outlaw alcohol in 1880, and would not receive its modern conservative reputation until the 1930s, when it was devastated by the Depression and the Dust Bowl. The slavery conflict would largely fade from Kansas cultural memory, except in the college town of Lawrence, which revels in its legacy as radical abolition's spiritual capital. Dominating Lawrence is the University of Kansas and its Jayhawk mascot, while "Free State" remains a self-bestowed Lawrence metonym.

The modern-day University of Kansas campus atop Lawrence's Mount Oread; lying out of view behind the ridge is the main downtown district Quantrill sacked in 1863. Although the 1855–65 Kansas–Missouri war has largely been forgotten by the rest of the country, the conflict remains the defining identity of towns like Lawrence, Osceola, and Centralia. (Photo by Brendan Costello. © The University of Kansas, 2023.)

THE BATTLEFIELDS TODAY

Certain areas of the 1864 Price campaign are rich with well-preserved Civil War and frontier history worth exploring. The St. Louis area has the Missouri Civil War Museum which is worth visiting. Meanwhile, the nearby Fort Davidson Battlefield has been preserved as the Battle of Pilot Knob State Historic Site.

Along the Missouri River area route Price took is the Battle of Lexington State Historic Site, as well as the town of Independence. Both Lexington and Independence were sites of earlier Civil War battles, and much of their historic preservation also commemorates these as well as the 1864 campaign. However, a major part of the October 22, 1864 battle of Independence took place on the future grounds of the iconic Independence Temple of the Community Church of Christ.

The battle of Westport, and its companion battle of Mine Creek, are strangely two of the most underreported battles of the American Civil War. The author, a lifelong, avid military history fan, grew up in southeast Kansas and has been intimately acquainted with Kansas City since birth, yet the battles are not part of local public school history curricula, or is the average or even mid-level amateur historian in the area typically aware of them.

A major reason for Westport's obscurity is that virtually all of the extended Westport battlefields have been built over with extensive residential and commercial development since 1864. Among the most prominent is Brush Creek, which has been canalized and now anchors Kansas City's high-end Country Club Plaza shopping and entertainment district.

Because the Westport engagement was such a sprawling battle, the surviving battlefields and monuments are located some distance from each other. The most prominent memorialization is the Battle of Westport Visitor Center in Kansas City's Loose Park, located in the 1855 Harris-Kearney House, home of the Westport Historical Society. The Visitor Center normally requires a scheduled reservation to be toured. However, there is also a self-guided automobile tour which will take the visitor around the Kansas City area to significant points of engagement, such as Byram's Ford.

One can also follow Price's October 24–25 retreat south through Kansas. Just outside Pleasanton, Kansas, is the Mine Creek Civil War Battlefield, preserved by the Kansas State Historical Society. Not far from Mine Creek, the Fort Scott National Historic Site, in the town of Fort Scott, Kansas, has been preserved by the National Park Service as a Frontier/Civil War-era US Army cavalry fort.

SELECT BIBLIOGRAPHY

Bird, Roy Dean, *They Deserved a Better Fate: The Second Kansas State Militia Regiment and the Price Raid, 1864*, Cummings & Hathaway (1999)

Bird, Roy, *Civil War in Kansas*, Pelican Publishing Company (2024)

Britton, Wiley, *The Civil War on the Border, Volume II 1863–1865*, G.P. Putnam's Sons (1899)

Buresh, Lamir F., *October 25th and the Battle of Mine Creek*, Lowell Press (1977)

Castel, Albert Edward, *A Frontier State at War: Kansas, 1861–1865*, Cornell Press (1958)

Castel, Albert, *General Sterling Price and the Civil War in the West*, LSU Press (1993)

Chinn, Jennie, *The Kansas Journey*, Gibbs Smith (2005)

Cody, Colonel William F., *The Life and Adventures of Buffalo Bill*, Harper & Brothers (1904)

Collins, Jr., Charles D., *Battlefield Atlas of Price's Missouri Expedition of 1864*, Combat Studies Institute Press (2016)

Coggins, Jack, *Arms and Equipment of the Civil War*, Dover Publications, Inc. (2004)

Davis, Major Dale E., "Guerrilla Operations in the Civil War: Assessing Compound Warfare during Price's Raid" (2004)

Erath, John, "Union Success in the Civil War and Lessons for Strategic Leaders" in *Joint Force Quarterly 77, 2nd Quarter* (2015)

Gilmore, Donald L., *Civil War on the Missouri-Kansas Border*, Pelican Publishing Company (2008)

Jenkins, Paul B., *The Battle of Westport*, Franklin Hudson Publishing Co. (1906)

Katcher, Philip, *Union Cavalryman 1861–65*, Osprey Publishing (2013)

Lee, Fred L., *The Battle of Westport, October 21–23, 1864*, Westport Historical Society (1976)

McLachlan, Sean, *American Civil War Guerrilla Tactics*, Osprey Publishing (2009)

Monaghan, Jay, *Civil War on the Western Border 1854–1865*, Literary Licensing LLC (2012)

Monnett, Howard N., *Action before Westport, Revised Edition*, University Press of Colorado (1995)

Price, Sterling, *Report of Major General Sterling Price: Price's Missouri Expedition* (1864)

Websites:

http://www.battleofwestport.org/

http://www.civilwaronthewesternborder.org/

http://www.kshs.org/

INDEX

Figures in **bold** refer to illustrations.

ammunition supplies 55, 57, **60**, 63, 72
Anderson, William "Bloody Bill" 4, 23, 25–26, 44, **45**, **46**, 48, 49, 89, **89**, 90

Battle of Albany (October 26, 1864) 89
Battle of Baxter Springs (October 6, 1863) 27
Battle of Boonville (June 17, 1861) 21, 25
Battle of Brandy Station (June 9, 1863) 6
Battle of Brush Creek (October 23, 1864) 23, **71**, 71–72, **72**, **75**, 76–81, **77**, **79**, **90**, 93
Battle of Byram's Ford (Big Blue River) (October 22, 1864) 22, 23, 72–76, **73**, **74**, **75**
Battle of Chickamauga (September 1863) 26, **27**
Battle of Corinth (1862) **27**
Battle of Fort Davidson (September 27–28, 1864) 22, 38–41, **39**, **40**, 51, 93
Battle of Gettysburg (July 1863) 17
Battle of Glasgow (October 15, 1864) 22, 48–49
Battle of Independence (October 21, 1864) 22, 57–63, **58–59**, **60**, **62**, **75**, 93
Battle of Iuka (September 19, 1862) **27**
Battle of Lexington (October 19, 1864) 22, 54–55, 93
Battle of Little Blue River (October 21, 1864) 22, 55–57, **74**
Battle of Marais des Cygnes (October 25, 1864) **55**, 82
Battle of Marks' Mills (April 25, 1864) **25**
Battle of Marmiton River (October 25, 1864) 88–89
Battle of Mine Creek (October 25, 1864) 4, 6, 23, 26, 82–88, **83**, **84–85**, **86**, **87**, **88**, 91, 93
Battle of Newtonia (October 28, 1864) 23, 89–90
Battle of Pea Ridge (March 7–8, 1862) **12**, 13, 21, 24, **27**
Battle of Prairie Grove (December 7, 1862) 21
Battle of Sedalia (October 15, 1864) 22, 49–50
Battle of the Big Blue River (October 22, 1864) 63–71, **65**, **74**
  at Mockbee Farm **2**, 66, **67**, **68–69**, **70**, **74**
Battle of Westport (October 22–23, 1864) 22, 28, **28**, **52**, **74–75**, **78**, **80**, **81**, 91, 93
Battle of Wilson's Creek (August 10, 1861) 12, 21, 24
Baxter Springs Massacre 22, 92
Benteen, Lt Col Frederick W. 4, 63, 76, **76**, 87
Blair, Col Charles W. 53, 64, 71, 77, 78, **78**
"Bleeding Kansas" and territorial warfare 8–10, 13, 29
Blunt, Maj Gen James G. 17, 27, 30, 50, 51–53, **52**, 54, 55, 57, **60**, 61, 64, 65, 66, 67, **75**, 77, 78, 81, 82
"Border Ruffians" of Missouri 8, 9–10, 29
Brown, Brig Gen Egbert 43, 47, 55, 63, 72
Burnes, Capt Ross 66, 67, **70**
"Burnt District" 16, **39**

Cabell, Brig Gen William 62, 63, 88
Carney, Governor Thomas 22, 23, 27, **36**, 51, **51**, 52, 53, 56, 64, 92
Centralia Massacre 22, 26, 46
Cheyenne War (July 1864) 36, 50, 51, **51**, 92
Clark, Brig Gen John B. **48**, 48–49, 50, 56
Cody, Pte William F. "Buffalo Bill" 4, 30, **43**
Confederate Army 4, 6, 10, **11**, 12, **12**, 13, 14, 17, 19, 21, 24, **32**, 36, **84–85**, **86**, 87–88, **90**, 92
  Army of Missouri 22, 24, 25, 28, 29, 31, **34**, 35, 37, 41, 42, 43, 44, 47, 48, 49–50, 54, 56, 61, 63, 71, **74**, **75**, 81, 82, **88**, 89, 90
  Army of Northern Virginia 19, 36, 42
  brigades **13**, 88
    Cabell 41, 62, 71, 75
    Clark 48, 54, 56, 72, 76, 82
    Freeman 58–59, 60, 76
    Iron Brigade (Shelby/Thompson) 6, 25, 37, 43, 47, 47, 54, 57, 65, 66, 67, 70, 74, 78, 80, 88
    Jackman 48, 57, 64–65, 66, 70, 74, 77, 78, 80, 88
    Slemons 62, 75
  divisions 29
    Fagan 28, 37, 38, 39, 41, 47–48, 54, 61, 62, 71, 72, **75**, 80, 82, 87, 88
    Marmaduke 25, 28, 37, 38, 39, 41, 42, 43, 47–48, 54, 57, 61, 62, 71, 72, **74**, **75**, 82, 87, 88
    Shelby 25, 28, 37, 38, 43, 48, 54, 56, 57, **58–59**, **60**, 61, 71, 72, **75**, 77, 82, 88, 89
  regiments 28–29, 56, 63, 80
    5th Missouri 66, **68–69**, **70**
Confederate government 11, 12, 17, **20**, 21
  Trans-Mississippi Department 24
Confederate Missouri shadow government 13, 24, 35, 44
Confederate strategy 17, 19–20, 23, 35, 37–38, 39–42, 44, 47–48, 50, 54–55, 56, **60**, 61, 64–65, 66–67, 71, 76, 78, 81–82, 87, 88
Crawford, Col Samuel J. 23, 51, 92
Curtis, Brig Gen Samuel R. **12**, 13, **14**, 22, 23, 27, **27**, 30, 36, 50–51, 52, 53–54, 55–56, 57, **60**, 61–62, 63–64, 65, 66, 67, 71, **75**, 76–77, 78, **78**, 80, **80**, 81, 82, 89

Davis, President Jefferson 19, **20**, 24
Deitzler, Maj Gen George W. 27, 30, 52, 53, 64, **65**, 67, 71, 77
Democratic Party 17, **19**

EMM (Enrolled Missouri Militia) 31, 41, 42, 43
  8th Provisional 82
  33rd EMM 89
Ewing, Brig Gen Thomas J., Jr. 16, 26, 38, 39, **39**, 41

Fagan, Maj Gen James F. 25, **25**, 38
Federal strategy 17–19, **20**, 35–36, **36**, 37, 38, 41, 42–44, 46–47, 50, 51–57, 61–64, 65–66, 67–71, **71**, 72–77, **74**, 78, 80, 81–82, 87, 89
Federal US Army forces 6, 9, 11, 12, 14, 15, 17, **17**, 23, 29, **32–33**, 39, 46, 48, 49, **84–85**, **86**, 92
  armies 13, 19, 26, 47
    Army of the Border 27, 30, 50, 61, 64, 67, 71, 72
    Army of the Department of Missouri 30, 55, 57, 71, 72
  brigades
    Kansas 43, 47, 87, 88
      1st 53, 54, 64, 65, 66, 67, 71, 72, 74, 75, 78, 89
      2nd 53, 54–55, 56, 57, 57, 64, 66, 67
      3rd 53, 64, 71, 77, 78, 78
      4th 64, 65, 67, 71, 75, 78, 89
    Missouri
      1st 55, 63, 72, 87, 88
      2nd 55, 62, 63, 72, 75, 88
      3rd 55, 55, 62, 63, 72, 75, 76, 82, 88
      4th 55, 63, 72, 73, 75, 80, 87, 88
  divisions 50
    Kansas Provisional Cavalry Division 30, 53, 55, 57, 61, 62, 64, 75, 81
    Missouri Provisional Cavalry 26, 27, 30, 50, 71, 72, 75, 81
  regiments 13, 15, 26, 38, 47
    1st Kansas 25, 27
    2nd Arkansas 63, 82

2nd Colorado Volunteer 51, 53, 67, 71, 72, 77, 82
2nd South Carolina 6, 53
3rd Iowa 63, 86
3rd Wisconsin Volunteer 51, 66
4th Iowa 76, 87, 88
7th Kansas 43, 62, 63, 72
10th Missouri 63, 76, 76, 87
11th Kansas 16–17, 30, 50–51, 53, 56, 57, 57, 60, 61, 74
13th Missouri 62, 63
14th Kansas 53, 78
15th Kansas 50–51, 53, 66, 66, 72, 80
16th Kansas 50–51, 57, 58–59, 60, 67
17th Illinois 62, 63
General Order No. 11 16, 16, 22, 39, 39, 50
XVI Corps 26, 30, 34, 37, 38, 41, 43, 44, 50, 55, 61, 63
Ford, Col James H. 6, 53, 64, 67
Fort Leavenworth, Kansas 9, 35, 50, 51, 53
Fort Scott, Kansas 35, 93
Freeman, Col Thomas R. **60**, 72, **73**, 76

Gordon, Col Frank 66, 67, **70**
Grant, Brig Gen Melvin 64, 65, 66, 67, 89
Grant, Lt Gen Ulysses S. 17, 19, **20**, 26, **27**, 35–36, 55, 91–92

Halleck, Maj Gen Henry 15, 36, 55
Hickok, James "Wild Bill" 4, 42, **42**, **43**
Hindman, Maj Gen Thomas 13, 15

Jackman, Col Sidney D. 48, 49, 66, 67
Jackson, Claiborne Fox 11, 12, 13, 21
James, Frank and Jesse 4, 29, 44, 46, **46**
Jennison, Lt Col Charles R. "Doc" 6, 14, 15, **15**, 53, 64, 65, 66, **66**, 67, **72**, 80
Johnson, Jeremiah "Liver-Eating" 4, **72**

Kansas and the Union 10, 21
Kansas City, Missouri **4**, 35, **80**, **81**, **90**, 92, 93
Kansas Free State 8, 9, 10
Kansas Jayhawkers 6, 14, **15**, 16, **16**, 21, 51, **53**, **72**, 82
Kansas–Missouri "Border War" (1861–64) 13–17, **15**, **16**, 26
Kansas Territory 7–8, **8**

Lane, Senator James H. "Jim" 6, 8, 14, **14**, 15, 16, 27, **36**, 51, **51**, 52
Lawrence Massacre 15, **16**, 21, 92
Lee, Gen Robert E. 19, 36, 42
Lincoln, President Abraham 10, 12, 17, 19, **19**, 21, 23, 36, 92
Little Dixie region, Missouri 7, 8, 12, 24, **25**
Lyon, Capt Nathaniel 11, 12, 21

Marais des Cygnes Massacre 9–10
Marmaduke, Maj Gen John S. 7, 13, **25**, 56, 76, 88
martial law in Kansas 22, 52, 81
McLain, Capt W.D. 57, 67, 78
McNeil, Brig Gen John 13, 42–43, 47, 55, 62–63, 80–81
Mexican–American War (1846–48) 7, 24, **25**, 27
military strengths and complements 28, 29, 30, 31, 38, 39, 43, 50, 52, 53, 54, 55, 62, 63–64, 71, 89
Missouri and the Union 10–11, 12, 21, 92
Missouri Bushwhackers 15, 16, 17, 21, 25, 29, 44–46, **45**, 49, 89, 90
Missouri Expedition (Price's Raid) (September–October 1864) 4, 20, 24, 25, 27, 35, 37–41, **40**, 47–48, 89–90, 91, **91**
Jefferson City, Missouri 42–44
and Kansas 50–51, 52, 54, 64
Montgomery, Col James H. 6, 14, 53, **53**
Moonlight, Col Thomas 53, 54, 56, 57, **57**, **60**, **61**, 62, 64, 66, 67, **74**
MSG (Missouri State Guard) 11, 12, 13, 24, 25, 29, **47**, **54**

Nebraska Territory 7

Ozarks 34–35, **34**, **39**

Partisan Ranger Act (Confederate, 1862) 15, **17**
Philips, Col John **75**, 76, 82, **86**, 87
Pierce, President Franklin 8, 9
Pleasonton, Maj Gen Alfred S. 6, 26, 46–47, **47**, 49, 50, 55, 57, 61–62, 63, 71, 72–76, **75**, 80, 81, 82, 87
plunder and pillage 14, 29, 42, 46, 47, 49, 52, 77, 82
population settlement and trends 6–7, 10, 92
presidential election (1864) 17, 19, **19**, 23, 92
Price, Maj Gen Sterling **5**, **7**, 11, 12, 20, 22, 23, 24, 25, 26, 28, 29, 31, 35, 37, 38, 39, 41–42, 44, **46**, 47–48, 49, 50, 51, **51**, 52, 53, **54**, 54–55, 56, 61, 63, 64–65, 71, 80, 81–87, 88, 89, **89**, 90, 91
Price–Harney Truce 11–12
prisoners 9, 11, 48, 49, 80, 82, **87**, 88

Quantrill, William C. 4, 17, **26**, 44, 48, 49, 90
Quantrill's Raiders 14–15, **16**, 17, **17**, 21, 25, 44, 89

Reader, 2nd Lt Samuel J. **31**, **64**, 67, **67**, **87**, **91**
Red River campaign 19, 22, 29
Republican Party 17, **19**, 51
Reynolds, Thomas C. 13, 24
Rosecrans, Maj Gen William S. 6, 26, **27**, 30, 31, 36, 37, 38, 42, 43, 46, 50, 51, 52, 53, 55, 57, 62, 63, 64, 71, 81

Sanborn, Brig Gen John **42**, 42–43, 47, 48, 49, 50, 54, 55, **55**, 62–63, 76, 82, 89
scouts 30, 38, 42, **42**, **43**, **51**, 53, 62, 63, 66
Shelby, Brig Gen Joseph "Jo" 6, 7, 13, **13**, 25, 38, 39, 64, 65, 66, **70**, **74**, **75**, 77, 78, 80, 88
Shelby's Raid (August–November 1863) 13, 22
Sherman, Maj Gen William T. 19, 91–92
slave states and the Union 6, 10, 34–35, 78, 92
Slemons, Col William 62, 88
Smith, Gen E. Kirby 19–20, **20**, 22, 24, 35, 37
Smith, Maj Gen Andrew Jackson (A.J.) 26, 30, 37, 38, 43, **44**, 50, 55, 61–62, 63

terrain 34, **34**, 35, 39, 76, 77, **86**
Thoman, George **75**, 77
Thompson, Brig Gen M. Jeff 47, **47**, 49, 50, 67, **70**
Todd, Lt George 26, 44, 46, 63, 90
training 28, 41, 42, 43, **64**
Trans-Mississippi Theater **20**, 29, 35

Union militias 12, 13, 38
KSM (Kansas State Militia) 27, 30, 31, 31, 51, 52, 53, 54, 56, 64, 64, 65, 65, 66, 67, 71, 72, 77, 78
2nd KSM **2**, 62, 66, 67, **67**, **68–69**, **70**, **74**
MSM (Missouri State Militia) 11, 31
US War Department 26
Department of Kansas 26–27, 29, 30, 36, 50, 51, 52
Department of Missouri 26, 29, 36, 38, 52, 54, 55

weaponry 30, **31**, **68–69**, **70**, 78, **81**, **84–85**, **86**, 87
Winslow, Col Edward F. 50, 55, 63, 72, 76